Decoding Cryptocurrency

Navigating the Crypto Space: An Introduction to Virtual Money and Blockchain Technology

Finnley Blake

Table of Contents

INTRODUCTION

Welcome to "Decoding Cryptocurrency: Navigating the Crypto Space - An Introduction to Virtual Money and Blockchain Technology." We explore the fascinating realm of cryptocurrencies and the innovative blockchain technology that powers them in this extensive book.

The emergence of cryptocurrencies in recent times has captivated the attention of individuals across the globe, upending established financial structures and creating novel opportunities for the evolution of money. The growing acceptance of cryptocurrencies such as Ethereum and Bitcoin has sparked debates about how they might change the way we conduct financial transactions and how our economies operate.

This book seeks to provide a strong basis for comprehending these innovative ideas by demystifying the difficulties surrounding blockchain technology and cryptocurrency. This book is meant to be easily accessible, educational, and entertaining for all levels of investor, be they novices or seasoned pros wishing to expand their skills.

We start our investigation by examining the core principles of cryptocurrencies, including what they are, how they operate, and how they differ from conventional fiat money. You will learn about the background of cryptocurrencies and their remarkable rise to prominence as the first decentralized digital currency, Bitcoin.

It is essential to comprehend the underlying technology to see the potential of cryptocurrencies fully. We delve into the complexities of blockchain technology, the foundation of the whole cryptocurrency ecosystem, in this book. We establish the foundation for understanding the workings of safe and open transactions, from mining and consensus algorithms to wallets and private keys.

Now that we are aware of the fundamentals, we can turn our attention to the fascinating realm of cryptocurrency investing. We cover essential topics such as assessing the benefits and drawbacks, recognizing market trends, and creating wise investment plans, enabling you to make wise choices in this volatile and always-changing market.

Furthermore, regulatory agencies are becoming increasingly interested in cryptocurrencies as they continue to gain popularity. We look into how cryptocurrency laws are changing worldwide and what that can mean for investors and consumers alike. Tax implications for cryptocurrency transactions are also significant for maintaining compliance and protecting your capital.

When navigating the crypto realm, security and risk management are essential. We explore common security risks and provide you with best practices to protect your digital assets and avoid fraud and scams that might infect the sector.

In addition to being used as investment vehicles, cryptocurrencies are increasingly being used in practical settings. We look at various application scenarios, from routine transactions to their function in international payments and remittances. We also examine the novel idea of decentralized finance (DeFi) and its potential to revolutionize established financial systems.

We consider the future state of the cryptocurrency industry as the globe observes its continuous progress. By addressing possible obstacles, new developments, and the effects of central bank digital currencies (CBDCs), we hope to bring you a forward-thinking viewpoint that piques your interest and encourages analysis.

Blockchain technology has a much wider impact than just cryptocurrency. In a dedicated chapter, we examine its wider applications in supply chain management, healthcare, and other industries, emphasizing the possibility of revolutionary transformation in several fields.

We intend for you to thoroughly understand blockchain technology and cryptocurrency fundamentals by the time you finish reading this book. We hope this book will serve as your compass in navigating the fascinating and constantly evolving crypto field, whether it inspires you to invest, investigate cutting-edge solutions, or broaden your knowledge.

So, without further ado, let's embark on this fascinating journey into the realm of blockchain technology and cryptocurrencies, where virtual money meets the limitless possibilities of the future.

CHAPTER I

Understanding Cryptocurrencies

What are cryptocurrencies?

The term "cryptocurrencies," which was created by combining the words "crypto" and "currencies," refers to a revolutionary development in the fields of technology and finance. Cryptocurrencies, which emerged from the 2008 financial crisis and were made widely known with the introduction of Bitcoin, have quickly become well- known and captivated the interest of people, companies, and investors worldwide. In this section, we will delve into the fundamental nature of cryptocurrencies, exploring their definition, key characteristics, and the groundbreaking technology that powers them.

At its core, cryptocurrency is a form of digital or virtual currency that relies on cryptographic techniques for secure and efficient financial transactions. Unlike traditional fiat currencies issued and regulated by governments, cryptocurrencies are decentralized systems built on a technology known as blockchain. The term "blockchain" refers to a distributed and immutable ledger that records all transactions across a network of computers, ensuring transparency and preventing double-spending. The genesis of cryptocurrencies can be traced back to the enigmatic figure of Satoshi Nakamoto, who introduced Bitcoin in 2008, a whitepaper with title of "Bitcoin: A Peer-to-Peer Electronic Cash System." Bitcoin, the first-ever cryptocurrency, was released as an open- source software in 2009, marking the birth of a transformative financial phenomenon.

One of the defining characteristics of cryptocurrencies is their decentralized nature. Traditional currencies rely on centralized institutions like banks and governments to oversee transactions and maintain records. In contrast, cryptocurrencies operate on decentralized networks of computers (nodes) that collectively validate and record transactions. This decentralization guarantees that no single entity controls the entire system, making cryptocurrencies resilient to censorship and single points of failure.

Cryptocurrencies leverage cryptographic techniques to secure transactions and protect users' digital assets. Each transaction is encrypted and connected to the previous one, forming a chain of blocks, hence the term "blockchain." This chain makes altering past transactions practically impossible, enhancing the security and integrity of the overall system.

While transactions recorded on the blockchain are transparent and accessible to all, the participants' identities are usually represented by cryptographic addresses rather than personal information. This pseudonymous nature provides users a certain degree of privacy, although it has also raised concerns about potential misuse for illegal activities.

Many cryptocurrencies, including Bitcoin, have a predetermined maximum supply, creating a scarcity aspect similar to precious metals like gold. For example, there will only ever be 21 million Bitcoins in existence. This limited supply is programmed into the cryptocurrency's code and helps protect against inflation, making them potentially attractive as a store of value.

Cryptocurrencies transcend geographical boundaries, enabling individuals worldwide to participate in the network. With internet access and a digital wallet, people can send, receive, and store cryptocurrencies without traditional banking infrastructure.

At the heart of every cryptocurrency lies the revolutionary technology called blockchain. Blockchain, a decentralized and distributed ledger that ensures secure, transparent, and immutable record-keeping of all transactions within the cryptocurrency network. The blockchain achieves this through a series of blocks, each has a list of transactions, and these blocks are linked together in chronological order, forming a continuous chain.

Cryptocurrencies rely on various consensus mechanisms to maintain the integrity of the blockchain and ensure consensus among network participants. One of the most widely used mechanisms is Proof-of-Work (PoW), used by Bitcoin and many others. In PoW, miners compete to solve complicated mathematical puzzles, and the first to solve it gets to add a new block to the blockchain, while also receiving a reward in the form of freshly minted coins and transaction fees. This process makes creating new blocks computationally intensive and requires significant computational power.

Another consensus mechanism gaining popularity is Proof-of-Stake (PoS). In PoS, validators are selected to create new blocks depending on the number of coins they "stake" or lock up as collateral. PoS is considered more energy-efficient than PoW since it doesn't require miners to solve complex puzzles but rather stake their coins.

Cryptocurrencies have found many applications beyond being a digital asset or a medium of exchange. For instance, they have become popular for remittances, allowing individuals to send money across borders more quickly and at lower costs than traditional banking methods. Moreover, cryptocurrencies have paved the way for the emergence of decentralized finance (DeFi) applications, which aim to recreate traditional financial services using blockchain technology, cutting out intermediaries and reducing transaction costs.

While cryptocurrencies have achieved substantial success, they also face challenges. Volatility remains a primary concern, as their prices can experience significant fluctuations, leading to potential investment risks. Additionally, the regulatory landscape surrounding cryptocurrencies is continually evolving, with governments and financial authorities worldwide grappling to develop appropriate frameworks to balance innovation, security, and consumer protection.

Looking ahead, the prospects for cryptocurrencies are promising. As technology advances and adoption increases, cryptocurrencies may become more smoothly integrated into our daily lives, transforming how we transact, invest, and store value. Furthermore, ongoing research and development in blockchain technology hold the potential to address scalability, energy consumption, and privacy concerns, opening up new possibilities for the financial ecosystem.

In conclusion, cryptocurrencies represent a disruptive force in finance, introducing novel concepts such as decentralization, cryptographic security, and global accessibility. Powered by the revolutionary technology of blockchain, cryptocurrencies have transcended traditional boundaries, enabling peer-to-peer transactions across the globe. As they continue to evolve, cryptocurrencies reshape our understanding of money, finance, and the fabric of our economic systems. While challenges lie ahead, the journey of cryptocurrencies has only just begun, and the potential for transformative change remains vast, making them an essential topic of study and exploration in the modern era.

Historical background and the origins of Bitcoin

The rise of cryptocurrencies has been one of the most significant financial developments of the 21st century. Among them, Bitcoin stands as a pioneer and a symbol of the revolutionary potential of virtual currencies. This section will navigate the historical background and delve into the origins of Bitcoin, tracing its roots back to the mysterious figure of Satoshi Nakamoto and the events that led to the creation of the world's first decentralized digital currency.

The story of Bitcoin began with the events of the global financial crisis in 2008. October 31, 2008 saw the publishing of a whitepaper with a title of "Bitcoin: A Peer-to-Peer Electronic Cash System" by a group using the alias "Satoshi Nakamoto." This document outlined the blueprint for a new form of currency and payment system that operated without the need for centralized intermediaries such as banks or governments. The timing of the whitepaper was no coincidence; it arrived as public confidence in traditional financial institutions had eroded, and there was a growing interest in exploring alternative means of exchange and store of value.

Despite the groundbreaking nature of the whitepaper and its subsequent impact on the financial world, Satoshi Nakamoto's identity remains unsurprising. Whether Nakamoto is an individual or a group of people is still unknown. Throughout the years, many individuals have been speculated to be the mastermind behind Bitcoin, but none have been conclusively proven to be Nakamoto. The enigmatic figure's decision to maintain anonymity has only added to the allure and intrigue surrounding Bitcoin's origins.

On January 3, 2009, Nakamoto successfully mined the first block of the Bitcoin network, which is now referred to as the "genesis block" or "block 0." With the publication of this block, the Bitcoin network was formally introduced to the world. A message that embodied the spirit of the times was hidden within the data of this block. "The Times 03/Jan/2009 Chancellor on brink of a second bailout for banks," the message stated. This message alluded to a headline from The Times, a British newspaper, which reported on the government's efforts to bail out struggling banks during the financial crisis. It was a commentary on the traditional financial system's failings and a nod to Bitcoin's potential as an alternative.

One key innovation Nakamoto introduced was the consensus mechanism known as Proof-of-Work (PoW). PoW serves as the backbone of Bitcoin's security and decentralization. In the PoW system, miners compete to solve complicated mathematical puzzles, and the first one to find a valid solution gets the right to add the next block to the blockchain. This process secures the network and incentivizes miners through the reward of newly minted Bitcoins. As more miners participate in the network, the difficulty of the puzzles adjusts to maintain a steady rate of block creation.

In its infancy, Bitcoin attracted a small community of enthusiasts and early adopters intrigued by the concept of decentralized money. Transactions in the early days were sparse, with a few notable instances of Bitcoin being used to purchase goods and services online. One of the most famous early transactions involved the purchase of two Papa John's pizzas for 10,000 Bitcoins in May 2010. At the time, the value of 10,000 Bitcoins was relatively insignificant, but in hindsight, it highlights the immense appreciation in the value of Bitcoin over the years.

Bitcoin gained early notoriety due to its association with the dark web marketplace known as the Silk Road. Launched in 2011, the Silk Road provided a platform for illegal drug trade and other illicit activities using Bitcoin as its preferred payment method. The anonymity offered by Bitcoin transactions made it attractive for those seeking to avoid detection. Law enforcement ultimately shut down the Silk Road in 2013, leading to a temporary drop in the value of Bitcoin as concerns about its association with criminal activities surfaced.

As Bitcoin's user base expanded, its value surged, garnering attention from mainstream media and financial institutions. The cryptocurrency's price volatility also became apparent, with dramatic price swings becoming a hallmark of its market behavior. In 2017, Bitcoin experienced an unprecedented price rally, reaching an all-time high of almosy $20,000 in December of that year. However, the euphoria was short-lived, and the market witnessed a significant correction in the following months.

The quick development of Bitcoin and other cryptocurrencies caught the attention of governments and regulatory authorities worldwide. Concerns about potential risks such as money laundering, tax evasion, and fraud prompted various countries to implement regulations or outright bans on cryptocurrency trading and usage. The regulatory landscape continues to evolve, with some nations embracing cryptocurrencies and blockchain technology, while others remain cautious or prohibitive.

In recent years, Bitcoin has seen increased interest from institutional investors and financial institutions. The growing adoption of Bitcoin as a store of value and a hedge against inflation has led to the emergence of various financial products and services. For example, introducing Bitcoin futures contracts on major exchanges allows investors to speculate on the price movement without owning the underlying asset. Investment funds and asset managers have also started offering cryptocurrency exposure to their clients.

Another critical aspect of Bitcoin's history is its built-in mechanism for controlling its supply. Every 210,000 blocks mined, the block reward that miners receive is halved. This event, known as the "halving," occurs approximately every four years and significantly impacts the issuance rate of new Bitcoins. The halving events and growing demand have historically contributed to Bitcoin's upward price trends.

The success and significance of Bitcoin have extended far beyond its status as a digital currency. Its creation paved the way for the developing thousands of other cryptocurrencies, each with unique features and use cases. Bitcoin's open-source nature inspired a global community of developers and innovators to build upon its foundation, leading to the evolution of blockchain technology and the creation of decentralized applications (dApps).

In conclusion, the historical background and origins of Bitcoin paint a captivating tale of innovation, intrigue, and disruption. Since its inception as a response to the financial crisis, Bitcoin has grown into a global phenomenon, challenging traditional financial systems and inspiring new ways of thinking about money and value. Its creator, Satoshi Nakamoto, remains an enigma, leaving behind a lasting legacy that has reshaped the financial landscape. As the world continues to navigate the evolving cryptocurrency ecosystem, Bitcoin's journey is a testament to the transformative power of decentralized technologies and their potential to reshape our future.

Key characteristics and benefits of cryptocurrencies

In the financial industry, cryptocurrencies have become a revolutionary force that is upending traditional ideas about value and money. These digital assets, which are supported by blockchain technology, differ from conventional fiat currencies in a number of special ways. In this section, we will explore the key characteristics of cryptocurrencies, including decentralization, security, transparency, and immutability. Additionally, we will discuss the various advantages they bring to individuals, businesses, and the global economy.

One of the most significant characteristics of cryptocurrencies is their decentralized nature. Unlike traditional fiat currencies, controlled and regulated by central authorities like governments and banks, cryptocurrencies operate on decentralized networks. These networks consist of multiple nodes (computers) spread across the globe, each maintaining a copy of the blockchain ledger. This decentralization eliminates the need for intermediaries and allows users to conduct peer-to-peer transactions directly, bypassing banks and payment processors. Cryptocurrencies promote financial autonomy by removing intermediaries, reducing the risk of censorship, and enhancing financial inclusivity, particularly in regions with insufficient access to traditional banking services.

Cryptocurrencies leverage cryptographic techniques to secure transactions and protect user data. Each transaction is encrypted and listed on the blockchain, a tamper-resistant ledger that stores a complete history of all transactions. The cryptographic nature of cryptocurrencies ensures the integrity and privacy of financial transactions, making them highly secure against fraudulent activities and hacks. Unlike traditional banking systems, which often fall victim to data breaches and cyberattacks, the decentralized nature of cryptocurrencies minimizes the risk of single points of failure, making them a more secure alternative for storing and transferring value.

Blockchain technology, the foundation of cryptocurrencies, enables transparent and traceable transactions. Every transaction ever executed on the blockchain can be viewed by anyone, providing high transparency and public accountability. This transparency helps in auditing financial records and preventing fraudulent activities, making manipulating the system without detection challenging for bad actors. Moreover, the transparent nature of cryptocurrencies enhances trust and credibility, as users can verify the authenticity and validity of transactions in real-time, ensuring a level of trust often lacking in traditional financial systems.

Once a transaction is recorded on the blockchain, it becomes immutable, meaning it cannot be altered or deleted. This feature ensures the permanent record-keeping of all transactions and provides an irrefutable history of ownership and value transfer. The immutability of the blockchain enhances the reliability and accuracy of financial records, reducing the risk of fraud and providing an efficient and tamper-proof system for financial transactions.

Traditional financial systems often involve multiple intermediaries and third-party service providers, leading to significant transaction costs for users. Cryptocurrencies eliminate the need for these intermediaries, allowing users to conduct peer-to-peer transactions directly. As a result, transaction fees associated with cryptocurrency payments are typically lower than traditional financial systems. This feature is particularly advantageous for cross-border transactions, as cryptocurrencies enable quick and cost-effective international transfers without the delays and high fees associated with conventional banking methods.

One of the most significant advantages of cryptocurrencies is their potential to promote financial inclusion. According to the World Bank, approximately 1.7 billions of individuals worldwide lack access to formal financial services. Cryptocurrencies provide an alternative means of accessing financial services, particularly for developing countries' unbanked and underbanked populations. With a smartphone and internet connectivity, individuals can create a digital wallet and participate in the global financial system, regardless of location or socioeconomic status. This inclusivity empowers individuals with greater control over their financial assets and economic opportunities, fostering economic growth and prosperity.

Traditional international money transfers often involve delays and high fees, especially when transferring funds across different currencies and financial institutions. Cryptocurrencies enable instant and borderless transactions, facilitating quick and cost-effective cross-border payments. This feature is particularly beneficial for businesses engaged in global trade and remittance services, as it eliminates the need for intermediaries and reduces the time and fees associated with traditional cross-border transactions.

Cryptocurrencies empower individuals with more significant financial sovereignty, enabling them to control their funds and transactions completely. Unlike traditional bank accounts, where financial institutions have the authority to freeze accounts or limit access to funds, cryptocurrencies are stored in digital wallets with private keys, known only to the wallet holder. This control over personal financial assets ensures greater security and protection against potential asset seizure or confiscation.

For investors, cryptocurrencies offer a unique asset class that complements traditional investment portfolios. As cryptocurrencies have demonstrated significant price appreciation over time, they present an opportunity for diversification and potential high returns. Cryptocurrency investments do not directly correlate with traditional financial markets, which provides a hedge against economic uncertainties and inflation. However, it is essential to recognize that the market for cryptocurrency is highly volatile, and investors should exercise caution and conduct a profound research before investing.

Cryptocurrencies and blockchain technology have sparked a wave of innovation and technological advancement across various industries. Beyond financial applications, blockchain technology is being explored for applications in supply chain management, healthcare, voting systems, intellectual property, and more. The decentralization and transparency offered by cryptocurrencies have inspired new ideas and solutions that aim to disrupt traditional business models and enhance efficiency in various sectors.

In conclusion, cryptocurrencies possess key characteristics that make them a transformative force in the financial world. Their decentralization, security, transparency, and immutability set them apart from traditional fiat currencies, offering a range of benefits to individuals, businesses, and the global economy. From empowering financial inclusion and reducing transaction costs to fostering innovation and technological advancement, cryptocurrencies have the potential to reshape the way we conduct financial transactions and interact with the global financial system. However, it is essential to recognize that the cryptocurrency space is still evolving, and its widespread adoption will depend on addressing regulatory challenges, scalability issues, and ensuring user education and security. As the journey of cryptocurrencies continues, it promises to be an exciting and transformative era for the future of finance.

Different types of cryptocurrencies (Bitcoin, Ethereum, etc.)

Cryptocurrencies have brought about a new era of decentralized digital assets that challenge traditional financial systems. The first and most well-known cryptocurrency, Bitcoin, paved the way for many other digital currencies with unique features and use cases. This section will explore the different types of cryptocurrencies, focusing on two of the most prominent examples: Bitcoin and Ethereum. Additionally, we will delve into various other cryptocurrencies, highlighting their key characteristics and roles in the evolving cryptocurrency landscape.

Bitcoin, introduced by the mysterious Satoshi Nakamoto in 2009, is the world's first cryptocurrency and remains the most significant by market capitalization and adoption. As the pioneer of decentralized digital currency, Bitcoin's primary use case is as a peer-to-peer electronic cash system, enabling users to send and receive value directly without intermediaries like banks. Bitcoin operates on a Proof-of-Work (PoW) consensus mechanism, where miners compete to validate transactions and add them to the blockchain. Its restricted supply of 21 million coins and the process of halving its block rewards approximately every four years contributes to its scarcity, akin to precious metals like gold. Bitcoin's success has paved the way for other cryptocurrencies and continues to be a store of value and a hedge against inflation.

Ethereum, created by Vitalik Buterin and launched in 2015, is a groundbreaking cryptocurrency that expands the possibilities beyond simple value transfer. It introduced the concept of smart contracts, self-executing contracts with predefined conditions written in code. These contracts enable developers to create decentralized applications (dApps) that run on the Ethereum blockchain, unlocking many potential use cases beyond financial transactions. Ethereum operates on a Proof-of-Work (PoW) consensus mechanism, similar to Bitcoin.

However, Ethereum is transitioning to Ethereum 2.0, which will employ Proof-of-Stake (PoS) to increase scalability and energy efficiency. Ethereum's versatile nature has led to its widespread adoption, fueling the growth of the decentralized finance (DeFi) ecosystem, non-fungible tokens (NFTs), and more.

Litecoin, created by Charlie Lee in 2011, is often called the "silver to Bitcoin's gold." It is a peer-to-peer cryptocurrency that shares many similarities with Bitcoin but offers specific improvements. Litecoin's key distinguishing feature is its faster block generation time of 2.5 minutes than Bitcoin's 10 minutes. This enables Litecoin to process transactions more quickly, making it more suitable for daily transactions. Like Bitcoin, Litecoin also uses PoW for consensus, and its overall supply is capped at 84 million coins, four times that of Bitcoin. While Litecoin has not achieved the same level of popularity as Bitcoin, it remains a respected and widely used cryptocurrency.

Ripple, developed by Ripple Labs in 2012, is a bridge currency for cross-border payments and remittances. Unlike most other cryptocurrencies, Ripple is not mined but pre-mined, with 100 billion XRP tokens created at its inception. Ripple's consensus mechanism, the Ripple Protocol Consensus Algorithm (RPCA), relies on a network of trusted validators to confirm transactions. This design allows Ripple to achieve high scalability and faster transaction times, making it an appealing choice for financial institutions seeking cost-effective and efficient cross-border transactions. Ripple's technology has gained significant attention from traditional financial institutions, making it one of the few cryptocurrencies with notable institutional adoption.

Cardano, launched in 2017 by Charles Hoskinson, is often hailed as a third-generation blockchain platform. It aims to address the scalability, sustainability, and interoperability issues of earlier blockchains like Bitcoin and Ethereum. Cardano operates on a PoS consensus mechanism called the Ouroboros protocol, which improves energy efficiency and enhances the network's security. One of Cardano's defining features is its focus on peer-reviewed academic research and scientific rigor to ensure the platform's robustness and security. Cardano's development is divided into distinct phases, each introducing new functionalities and improvements. As it progresses, Cardano aims to provide a comprehensive infrastructure for decentralized applications and enable real-world adoption of blockchain technology.

Polkadot, founded by Dr. Gavin Wood in 2016, is a multi-chain network that enables interoperability between various blockchains. Its unique architecture allows multiple blockchains, called parachains, to connect to the Polkadot network through a central relay chain. This interoperability promotes collaboration and data sharing between different blockchains, creating a cohesive ecosystem. Polkadot's DOT token is the native cryptocurrency, used for staking and governance within the network. Polkadot aims to overcome scalability challenges and foster innovation across different blockchain projects by facilitating seamless communication between blockchains.

Stellar, co-founded by Jed McCaleb in 2014, is a decentralized blockchain platform that offers fast and low-cost cross-border transactions, particularly for the unbanked and underbanked populations. Stellar's consensus algorithm, called the Stellar Consensus Protocol (SCP), enables quick transaction confirmations, making it ideal for microtransactions and remittances. Stellar's native asset, XLM, serves as both a bridge currency and an anti-spam mechanism to prevent network abuse. The platform's mission is to improve financial inclusion by connecting financial institutions, payment systems, and individuals securely and efficiently.

Binance Coin (BNB), launched by Binance Exchange in 2017, is a utility token that powers various functions within the Binance ecosystem. Initially released on the Ethereum blockchain as an ERC-20 token, BNB later transitioned to its blockchain called Binance Smart Chain (BSC). BNB is the native cryptocurrency for Binance, one of the largest cryptocurrency exchanges globally. Users can use BNB to pay for trading fees at a discounted rate, participate in token sales on the Binance Launchpad, and access various decentralized finance (DeFi) applications on the Binance Smart Chain.

In conclusion, cryptocurrencies are a diverse and rapidly evolving landscape. Bitcoin and Ethereum, as the two most prominent cryptocurrencies, have revolutionized the financial industry and paved the way for many other digital assets. Each cryptocurrency has unique characteristics, use cases, and consensus mechanisms, catering to different needs and objectives. From Bitcoin's position as a store of value to Ethereum's role as a smart contract platform and beyond, the diversity of cryptocurrencies presents a rich tapestry of innovation and potential. As the cryptocurrency market matures and gain broader acceptance, staying informed and exploring the numerous opportunities and possibilities this transformative technology offers is essential.

How cryptocurrencies differ from traditional fiat currencies

Cryptocurrencies have emerged as a disruptive force in the world of finance, challenging traditional fiat currencies that have been the cornerstone of global economies for centuries. Unlike fiat currencies, which are provided and controlled by central authorities like the governments and central banks, cryptocurrencies operate on decentralized networks powered by blockchain technology. In this section, we will explore the fundamental differences between cryptocurrencies and traditional fiat currencies, focusing on aspects such as issuance, governance, security, transparency, and the role of intermediaries.

One of the main difference between cryptocurrencies and traditional fiat currencies lies in their issuance and governance. Central authorities, typically governments and banks, create and regulate Fiat currencies. The supply of fiat money can be modified at the discretion of these authorities through monetary policy, such as quantitative easing or interest rate adjustments. Governments can print more money, leading to inflation or deflation, depending on the prevailing economic conditions.

On the other hand, cryptocurrencies are typically decentralized and have fixed or capped supplies. Bitcoin, for example, has a utmost supply of 21 million coins, and its issuance is governed by an algorithmic process called mining. New Bitcoins are "mined" as a reward for miners who validate transactions and add blocks to the blockchain. The issuance of new Bitcoins follows a predetermined schedule and is not subject to human discretion or control. This fixed supply and decentralized issuance mechanism create a level of scarcity and predictability that sets cryptocurrencies apart from fiat currencies.

Another key distinction between cryptocurrencies and fiat currencies is their level of security and immutability. Traditional fiat currencies rely on centralized banking systems, where transactions are recorded in central databases controlled by financial institutions. While these systems implement security measures, they are susceptible to hacks, data breaches, and unauthorized access.

In contrast, cryptocurrencies leverage cryptographic techniques and decentralized blockchain technology to guarantee the security and immutability of transactions. Each transaction is encrypted, and a consensus mechanism (such as Proof-of-Work or Proof-of-Stake) is employed to validate and add transactions to the blockchain. Once a transaction is recorded on the blockchain, it becomes immutable and cannot be altered or deleted. This tamper-resistant nature ensures the integrity and transparency of financial transactions, making cryptocurrencies a more secure option for digital exchanges.

Transparency and privacy are often seen as conflicting attributes in finance. Traditional fiat transactions are subject to varying degrees of transparency, depending on the financial system's regulations and reporting requirements. While governments and financial institutions can access transaction data, the privacy of individual users is generally protected through legal and institutional safeguards.

Cryptocurrencies, on the other hand, offer high transaction transparency. Every transaction is recorded on a public blockchain, visible to anyone with internet access. This transparent nature ensures a comprehensive and real-time record of all transactions, preventing fraud and enhancing public trust.

However, this transparency comes with a trade-off in terms of user privacy. Although wallet addresses are not directly linked to users' identities, the blockchain allows users to trace their transaction history. To address this concern, some cryptocurrencies, such as Monero and Zcash, employ privacy features that obscure transaction details to varying degrees. These privacy-focused cryptocurrencies offer users a degree of anonymity and confidentiality not present in most traditional fiat transactions.

Traditional financial transactions often involve intermediaries, such as banks, payment processors, and clearinghouses, to facilitate and verify exchanges. These intermediaries add a layer of complexity and cost to financial transactions. While they play a crucial role in maintaining the stability and security of traditional financial systems, they can also introduce delays and additional fees.

Cryptocurrencies eliminate the need for many intermediaries, allowing users to conduct peer-to-peer transactions directly. Blockchain technology acts as a decentralized ledger, enabling the verification and validation of transactions without the involvement of third-party intermediaries. This direct peer-to-peer model streamlines financial exchanges, reduces costs, and promotes financial autonomy.

Cross-border transactions have traditionally been associated with high fees and extended processing times. Traditional financial systems involve multiple intermediaries, each charging fees for their services, leading to significant costs for international transfers.

Cryptocurrencies solve these challenges by enabling fast and cost-effective cross-border transactions. The decentralized characteristic of cryptocurrencies allows users to send and receive funds directly, bypassing the traditional banking network. As a result, cross-border transactions conducted with cryptocurrencies are typically quicker and incur lower fees than traditional methods.

Additionally, cryptocurrencies offer accessibility to financial services for individuals in underserved regions without access to traditional banking systems. As long as users have internet connectivity and a digital wallet, they can participate in the global financial system through cryptocurrencies. This feature is specifically valuable in regions with limited access to traditional banking infrastructure, promoting financial inclusion and economic empowerment.

Cryptocurrencies are often characterized by their high price volatility. Unlike most traditional fiat currencies, which are relatively stable and backed by the economic strength of governments and central banks, cryptocurrencies are influenced by various factors, including market demand, investor sentiment, and technological advancements.

This volatility presents opportunities and risks for investors and users of cryptocurrencies. While significant price fluctuations can result in substantial profits for traders, they can also lead to significant losses. As a result, investing in cryptocurrencies requires careful consideration, risk management, and a long-term perspective.

In contrast, traditional fiat currencies are subject to economic policies and regulations that central banks and governments enforce. These measures aim to stabilize the value of fiat currencies and maintain price stability. Central banks can use interest rates, money supply, and foreign exchange interventions to manage inflation and stabilize their economies.

In conclusion, cryptocurrencies and traditional fiat currencies differ significantly in their issuance, governance, security, transparency, and the role of intermediaries. Cryptocurrencies operate on decentralized networks, offering fixed supplies, enhanced security, and transparency through blockchain technology. They eliminate the need for intermediaries, enabling fast and cost-effective cross-border transactions and promoting financial inclusion.

However, cryptocurrencies also exhibit high price volatility and present unique challenges related to user privacy and regulatory considerations. Traditional fiat currencies, backed by governments and central banks, benefit from price stability and the ability to implement monetary policies to manage economic conditions.

As the adoption of cryptocurrencies develops, it is essential to recognize both their transformative potential and the complexities they introduce to the global financial landscape. Balancing innovation and regulation will be crucial as cryptocurrencies become an increasingly integral part of the future of finance.

CHAPTER II

How Cryptocurrencies Work

The fundamentals of blockchain technology

Blockchain technology is a revolutionary innovation that will have a significant impact on numerous industries. Blockchain was first presented as the foundational technology underpinning the decentralized cryptocurrency Bitcoin, but it has since developed into an adaptable tool with uses not limited to digital currency. In this section, we will explore the fundamentals of blockchain technology, its key components, principles, and the transformative potential it holds in shaping the future of various sectors, including finance, supply chain, healthcare, and more.

At its core, blockchain is a distributed and immutable ledger that records transactions or data across a network of computers, known as nodes. Unlike traditional centralized databases, where a single authority controls the data, blockchain operates decentralized, ensuring transparency, security, and trust among participants. Each new transaction is bundled into a block and linked to the previous block through cryptographic hashing, creating an unbroken chain of blocks. This chain, hence the name "blockchain," continuously grows with each new block added to the network.

One key component of blockchain technology that distinguishes it from traditional systems is decentralization. In a decentralized network, no single entity controls the entire system. Instead, decision-making authority is distributed among a network of participants, each maintaining a copy of the blockchain. This redundancy enhances the network's resilience, as it continues to function even if some nodes fail or malicious actors attempt to disrupt the system.

To come to an agreement over the legitimacy of transactions and preserve the blockchain's integrity, a number of consensus mechanisms are used. Proof-of-Work (or PoW), Proof-of-Stake (or PoS), Delegated Proof-of-Stake (or DPoS), and Practical Byzantine Fault Tolerance (or PBFT) are examples of frequently utilized mechanisms. The goal of all consensus mechanisms is to guarantee that the majority of nodes agree on the legitimacy of new transactions prior to their inclusion in the blockchain, however each process has pros and downsides of its own.

Blockchain technology ensures high levels of security through cryptography. Each block contains a cryptographic hash, a unique identifier generated based on the data contained within the block. Any alteration to the data in the block would change its hash, disrupting the chain's continuity and immediately revealing the tampering attempt. As each block is linked to the previous one, any changes in one block would invalidate all subsequent blocks, making it digitally impossible to alter past records without consensus from most of the network.

The immutability of blockchain makes it an excellent tool for recording sensitive and critical information, such as financial transactions, legal contracts, and medical records. Once data is recorded on the blockchain, it becomes tamper-proof, providing an auditable trail of events and transactions.

The advent of smart contracts is one of the biggest developments in blockchain technology. Self-executing contracts with pre-established rules and conditions expressed in code are known as smart contracts. When the required conditions are fulfilled, they immediately take action, doing away with the need for middlemen or outside enforcement. One of the most well-known blockchain systems, Ethereum, invented the idea of smart contracts, which allowed programmers to create decentralized apps (dApps) with programmable features.

Smart contracts have vast potential in various industries, including finance, supply chain management, and decentralized governance. They enable transparent and trustless execution of agreements, reducing the risk of fraud and inefficiencies.

Blockchain networks can be categorized into two main types: public and private blockchains. As exemplified by Bitcoin and Ethereum, public blockchains are open and permissionless, allowing anyone to participate in the network, validate transactions, and add new blocks. Anyone can access the public blockchain's data and verify the transaction history.

On the other hand, private blockchains are restricted and require permission to join and participate. Organizations or consortiums typically use them internally, where data access and validation are limited to selected participants. Private blockchains offer increased privacy and control but sacrifice the level of decentralization achieved by public blockchains.

Scalability has been a significant challenge for blockchain technology. As the number of transactions and users on a blockchain network increases, so does the computational power and storage demand. For public blockchains like Bitcoin and Ethereum, achieving high throughput and low transaction fees without compromising security has been a constant research and development focus.

Several approaches, such as sharding, off-chain solutions, and layer-two protocols, have been proposed to address scalability concerns. As blockchain technology evolves, scalability remains a crucial area of innovation and improvement to ensure broader adoption across industries.

Blockchain technology's potential goes beyond cryptocurrencies and extends to various real-world applications. In the financial sector, blockchain can revolutionize payment systems, cross-border remittances, and the issuance of digital assets. Decentralized finance (DeFi) platforms built on blockchain enable users to access financial services without intermediaries.

In supply chain management, blockchain can drive efficiency, transparency, and traceability. By recording the entire supply chain journey on the blockchain, stakeholders can validate the origin and authenticity of products, reducing counterfeiting and ensuring ethical sourcing.

Healthcare can also benefit from blockchain's secure and interoperable nature. Blockchain-based electronic health records (EHRs) can improve data security and streamline access to patient information for healthcare providers.

Blockchain technology has become a transformative force with the potential to reshape various industries. Its decentralized, secure, and transparent nature solves long-standing finance, supply chain, healthcare challenges, and beyond. As the technology continues to mature and scalability concerns are addressed, we expect to see increased adoption and further innovation, unlocking the full potential of blockchain in the global economy. From cryptocurrencies to smart contracts and supply chain solutions, blockchain is poised to revolutionize how we conduct transactions, exchange information, and build trust in the digital age.

Cryptocurrency mining and consensus mechanisms

Cryptocurrency mining and consensus mechanisms are integral to blockchain technology, serving as the backbone of decentralized digital currencies. These mechanisms ensure the security, transparency, and immutability of transactions on blockchain networks. In this section, we will delve into the fundamentals of cryptocurrency mining and the various consensus mechanisms employed by different cryptocurrencies. We will explore the role of miners, the concept of Proof-of- Work (PoW), alternative consensus mechanisms like Proof-of-Stake (or PoS), Delegated Proof-of-Stake (or DPoS), and Practical Byzantine Fault Tolerance (or PBFT), and their respective strengths and limitations in securing blockchain networks.

Cryptocurrency mining is how new transactions are validated and added to the blockchain. In a decentralized blockchain network, transactions are submitted by users and grouped into blocks. Miners, the participants in the network, compete to solve complex cryptographic puzzles to validate the transactions and add the new block to the blockchain. The first miner to find the solution for the puzzle and broadcast the solution to the network gets rewarded with newly minted coins and transaction fees paid by users for their transactions to be included in the block. This process is known as "mining," and it is crucial in keeping the integrity and security of the blockchain.

Proof-of-Work (PoW) is the original consensus mechanism introduced by Satoshi Nakamoto in the Bitcoin whitepaper. It forms the foundation of Bitcoin and several other cryptocurrencies. PoW relies on computational power to secure the network and achieve consensus. To validate a block, miners must find a nonce, a random number that, when hashed with the block's data, produces a hash with a specific number of leading zeros. The difficulty of finding the correct nonce is adjusted regularly to ensure that blocks are mined at a consistent rate, typically every 10 minutes for Bitcoin.

PoW has been praised for its security and robustness, as it requires immense computational power to alter the blockchain's history. However, it also has its drawbacks, such as the high energy consumption associated with mining and the centralization of mining power in large mining pools.

To address the energy consumption and centralization issues of PoW, the Proof-of-Stake (PoS) consensus mechanism was introduced. PoS operates on the premise that the more coins a participant holds, the more mining power they have and the higher their chances of being selected to create a new block. In PoS, there is no competition to solve cryptographic puzzles, as the selection of the next block creator is based on the stake (number of coins) held by participants.

PoS has gained popularity due to its energy efficiency and reduced centralization risks. Validators (participants in PoS networks) are incentivized to act in the network's best interest, as they have a financial stake in the system. PoS also helps mitigate the risk of a 51% attack, where a single entity gains majority network control.

Delegated Proof-of-Stake (pr DPoS) is a variation of the PoS consensus mechanism that introduces a delegated election process. Instead of all stakeholders participating directly in block validation, DPoS networks elect a limited number of delegates to perform this task. These delegates, also known as block producers, validate transactions and add blocks to the blockchain.

DPoS aims to enhance the efficiency of block production by reducing the number of validators and achieving faster block confirmation times. DPoS networks can achieve higher transaction throughput and scalability by electing a smaller group of trusted nodes. However, DPoS has been criticized for potentially leading to centralization, as the power to elect delegates may become concentrated in the hands of a few influential stakeholders.

Practical Byzantine Fault Tolerance (PBFT) is a consensus mechanism designed to address the issue of reaching consensus in networks with faulty or malicious nodes. In traditional Byzantine Fault Tolerance (BFT) systems, all nodes in the network must concur on the validity of a transaction before it is considered confirmed. However, this approach can be slow and resource-intensive.

PBFT introduces a practical approach by allowing a majority vote to determine the validity of transactions. This means that the transaction is considered valid and confirmed as long as a certain number of nodes (usually two-thirds) in the network are honest and reach a consensus. PBFT is particularly well-suited for private blockchain networks with a known set of trusted participants.

Cryptocurrency mining and consensus mechanisms are the pillars of blockchain technology, enabling decentralized networks to achieve agreement and immutability. Proof-of-Work has been the pioneering consensus mechanism, providing robust security but consuming substantial energy. As the industry evolves, alternative mechanisms like Proof-of-Stake, Delegated Proof-of-Stake, and Practical Byzantine Fault Tolerance offer promising solutions to address energy efficiency, scalability, and decentralization challenges.

Each consensus mechanism has unique strengths and limitations, making it essential for developers and stakeholders to consider their blockchain projects' specific requirements and objectives. As the world embraces blockchain technology, ongoing research and innovation in consensus mechanisms will continue to shape the future of cryptocurrencies and decentralized applications, unlocking the full potential of this life-changing technology across various industries.

Wallets and private keys

In cryptocurrencies, digital wallets and private keys are pivotal in securing and managing users' assets. Unlike traditional financial systems, where physical wallets and signatures authenticate transactions, cryptocurrencies rely on cryptographic keys for ownership and access control. This section will explore the fundamentals of digital wallets, the significance of private keys, and the various types of wallets available to users. Understanding the relationship between wallets and private keys is essential for safely navigating the world of cryptocurrencies and safeguarding one's digital assets.

In cryptocurrencies, a digital wallet is a software application or hardware device that allows users to store, send, and receive digital assets. It acts as a user's interface to the blockchain network, enabling them to access and manage their cryptocurrencies. A digital wallet has two essential components: a public address and a private key.

The public address is a user's unique identifier on the blockchain network. Others can use a long string of alphanumeric characters to send cryptocurrencies to the wallet. Sharing the public address with others is safe, as it does not reveal any sensitive information.

However, the private key is the most critical component of a digital wallet. A random string of characters, like a complex password, serves as the cryptographic key to access and control the cryptocurrencies associated with the wallet's public address. The private key must be kept secure and never shared with anyone else. Losing or compromising the private key can permanently lose access to the digital assets in the wallet.

There are several types of digital wallets, each offering different levels of security, accessibility, and convenience. The main categories of wallets are software, hardware, and paper wallets.

Software wallets come in various forms, including desktop, mobile, and web-based wallets. Web-based wallets can be accessed using internet browsers, desktop wallets can be downloaded on users' computers, and mobile wallets are found on smartphones. These wallets are convenient for daily transactions and offer relatively easy cryptocurrency access. However, they are vulnerable to hacking, malware, and phishing attacks, as they are connected to the internet.

Hardware wallets are tangible devices explicitly designed for securely storing cryptocurrencies offline. They are considered one of the most secure options for long-term storage of digital assets. Hardware wallets generate and hold private keys within the device, keeping them isolated from online threats. Transactions are signed within the device, ensuring private keys are never exposed to the internet. The physical nature of hardware wallets also provides an added layer of protection against digital threats.

Paper wallets are a form of cold storage where a user's public and private keys are printed on paper. As they are entirely offline, paper wallets offer a high level of security against online attacks. However, they can be inconvenient to use for frequent transactions, as the process involves manually entering the private key when accessing or transferring funds.

As mentioned earlier, private keys are the cornerstone of cryptocurrency ownership and security. They are mathematically linked to a user's public address and allow the user to sign transactions, providing proof of ownership and enabling the movement of cryptocurrencies. Private keys must be generated randomly, and their length and complexity determine their strength against brute-force attacks.

Users must understand that private keys are not recoverable if lost or forgotten. Unlike traditional financial systems, where passwords can be reset through authentication processes, cryptocurrencies provide no central authority to retrieve lost private keys. As a result, users must take utmost care in securely storing and backing up their private keys.

The security of private keys is of paramount importance in the cryptocurrency space. Several best practices can be followed to safeguard private keys.

Users should use reliable methods to generate strong and unique private keys. Software wallets often employ secure random number generators to create private keys, while hardware wallets generate them internally. Hardware wallets are considered highly safe for this reason.

Hardware wallets are recommended for significant amounts of cryptocurrencies meant for long-term storage. Keeping private keys offline reduces the risk of exposure to online threats and hacking attempts.

Some wallets allow users to set up multi-factor authentication, adding an extra layer of security. Multi-factor authentication requires users to provide additional verification, such as a code from their mobile device, when accessing their wallet.

Users should regularly back up their private keys and keep them in secure locations, away from potential threats like fire, water damage, or theft. Hardware wallets often provide seed phrases, a series of words that can be utilized to restore access to the wallet in the event of loss or damage.

Phishing attacks are prevalent in the cryptocurrency space. Users should be cautious about sharing their private keys, seed phrases, or any sensitive information with unverified sources.

Digital wallets and private keys are fundamental elements of the cryptocurrency ecosystem, allowing users to store, send, and receive digital assets securely. Understanding the importance of private keys and implementing robust security measures are essential to protecting one's cryptocurrencies from theft, loss, or compromise. The different types of wallets, such as software, hardware, and paper wallets, offer varying levels of security and accessibility, catering to the diverse needs of cryptocurrency users. As the adoption of cryptocurrencies grows, continuous research and innovation in wallet technologies will be crucial in providing users with a smooth and secure experience in managing their digital assets.

Transactions and the role of public ledgers

Transactions lie at the heart of the cryptocurrency ecosystem, serving as the mechanism through which digital assets are transferred between users on a blockchain network. These transactions are recorded and publicly available on a decentralized ledger known as a public ledger or blockchain. In this section, we will delve into the fundamentals of cryptocurrency transactions, exploring their structure, security, and efficiency. Furthermore, we will examine the critical role of public ledgers in ensuring transparency, immutability, and trust in the world of cryptocurrencies.

Cryptocurrency transactions entail the transfer of digital assets between two or more parties on a blockchain network. Each transaction comprises essential components, including the sender's public address, the recipient's public address, the amount of digital assets being transferred, and transaction metadata. Cryptocurrency transactions are broadcasted to the network, where miners or validators verify their validity and group them into blocks. Once a block of transactions is confirmed, it is added to the blockchain, creating an indelible record of the transaction history.

Cryptocurrency transactions differ from traditional financial transactions in that they are peer-to-peer, direct, and do not depend on intermediaries like banks or payment processors. This direct nature enables faster settlement times and lower transaction fees than traditional financial systems.

At the cryptocurrency ecosystem's core lies the public ledger, which is an immutable record of all transactions across a blockchain network. Public ledgers ensure transparency and security by making transaction data publicly accessible to all network participants. Each participant can access a copy of the entire ledger, and new transactions are continuously added, creating a chronological chain of blocks.

The decentralized nature of public ledgers ensures that no single entity or authority controls the data, preventing manipulation or tampering. Transactions recorded on the public ledger cannot be altered, providing an auditable and trustworthy history of all cryptocurrency activities.

Public ledgers offer complete transparency to all participants in the blockchain network. Any user can view the full transaction history and trace the movement of digital assets from one address to another. This transparency fosters trust in the system, as users can independently verify the accuracy and authenticity of transactions.

Immutability is a critical feature of public ledgers. Once a transaction is recorded on the blockchain and confirmed through the consensus mechanism, it becomes a permanent and unchangeable part of the ledger. This immutability prevents fraudulent activities, as altering a single transaction would require the consensus of most network participants, which is practically unfeasible due to the decentralized nature of blockchain networks.

Public ledgers are secured through consensus mechanisms, which ensure that most participants agree on the validity of transactions prior they are added to the blockchain. The most widely used consensus mechanism is Proof-of-Work (PoW), where miners compete to solve complex cryptographic puzzles to verify transactions and then add them to the blockchain. The first miner to find the solution for the puzzle gets rewarded and adds the block to the chain.

Another popular consensus mechanism is Proof-of-Stake (PoS), where validators are chosen to create new blocks based on the number of digital assets they "stake" or hold in the network. PoS is considered more energy-efficient than PoW but requires a level of trust in validators' integrity and the network's overall security.

Delegated Proof-of-Stake (DPoS) is a variation of PoS where stakeholders vote to elect delegates responsible for block production and validation. DPoS aims to achieve faster transaction confirmations and higher scalability by reducing the number of validators.

Practical Byzantine Fault Tolerance (PBFT) is another consensus mechanism designed to achieve consensus in networks with faulty or malicious nodes. PBFT ensures that the majority of nodes must concur on the validity of a transaction before it is considered confirmed, offering fast and final transaction confirmation.

Public ledgers enhance transaction efficiency and scalability by eliminating the need for intermediaries and central authorities. Traditional financial systems often suffer from bottlenecks and delays due to the involvement of numerous intermediaries in transaction processing. In contrast, cryptocurrency transactions can be processed directly between users, reducing delays and associated fees.

However, achieving high throughput and scalability remains challenging for some blockchain networks. Public ledgers based on PoW consensus, like Bitcoin, can experience slow transaction times and higher fees during periods of high network activity. As the industry evolves, various solutions, including layer-two protocols and off-chain scaling solutions, are being explored to improve scalability without compromising security.

While public ledgers provide transparency and immutability, they also raise concerns about user privacy and anonymity. As all transactions are publicly accessible, anyone can trace the flow of digital assets and potentially link addresses to specific individuals or entities.

To address privacy concerns, various privacy-focused cryptocurrencies and protocols, such as Monero and Zcash, employ advanced cryptographic techniques to obfuscate transaction details and ensure user anonymity. These privacy features allow users to conduct transactions without exposing their identities or transaction amounts to the public ledger.

Cryptocurrency transactions and public ledgers are the backbone of the decentralized financial revolution. Transactions enable the seamless transfer of digital assets between users, while public ledgers ensure transparency, immutability, and trust by recording and publicly displaying all transactions across the blockchain network.

The decentralized nature of public ledgers, secured by consensus mechanisms like PoW, PoS, DPoS, and PBFT, prevents single points of failure and enhances the security and integrity of cryptocurrency networks. While public ledgers provide transparency and audibility, they also raise privacy concerns, developing privacy-focused cryptocurrencies and protocols.

As the cryptocurrency ecosystem evolves, ongoing research and development in consensus mechanisms and scalability solutions will pave the way for widespread adoption and the integration of blockchain technology into various industries. Ultimately, public ledgers will remain at the forefront of ensuring the reliability and transparency of transactions in the ever-expanding world of cryptocurrencies.

CHAPTER III

Investing in Cryptocurrencies

Evaluating the risks and rewards of cryptocurrency investments

Cryptocurrency investments have gained significant attention in recent years, attracting seasoned investors and newcomers to the world of digital assets. The allure of potentially high returns, decentralized networks, and cutting-edge technology has captivated many individuals seeking to diversify their investment portfolios. However, like any investment, cryptocurrency carries its own set of risks and rewards. This section will explore the factors investors should consider when evaluating the potential risks and rewards of investing in cryptocurrencies. Understanding these aspects, from price volatility and regulatory uncertainties to technological advancements and long-term potential, is crucial for making informed decisions in the dynamic and ever-evolving cryptocurrency market.

One of the defining characteristics of cryptocurrencies is their price volatility. Unlike traditional financial assets, which often exhibit more stable price movements, cryptocurrencies can experience drastic price fluctuations over short periods. The high volatility can present both opportunities and risks for investors. On one hand, significant price swings offer the potential for substantial profits within a short timeframe. Some investors have witnessed exponential investment growth during bull markets, where cryptocurrency prices surge rapidly. On the other hand, sharp declines during bear markets can lead to substantial losses. Therefore, investors must have a risk tolerance that aligns with the inherent volatility of the cryptocurrency market.

Regulatory uncertainty is another critical factor that investors must consider when evaluating cryptocurrency investments. The regulatory landscape surrounding cryptocurrencies varies significantly from country to country and is continually evolving. Governments and financial authorities are grappling with how to regulate this new asset class, leading to a complex and often ambiguous regulatory environment. Regulatory changes can impact cryptocurrencies' legality, trading, and taxation, potentially affecting their market value and overall adoption. Investors should stay informed about the latest regulatory developments in their respective jurisdictions and be prepared to adapt their investment strategies accordingly.

Cryptocurrency investments also expose investors to security risks, particularly concerning the safety of their digital assets. Since cryptocurrencies are digital and typically stored in online wallets or exchanges, they are susceptible to hacking and cyber attacks. Several high-profile incidents have resulted in losing millions of dollars worth of cryptocurrencies due to security breaches. Investors should prioritize the security of their wallets and exchanges by employing strong passwords, enabling two-factor authentication, and considering using hardware wallets for cold storage of their assets.

Market liquidity is another aspect that impacts the risks and rewards of cryptocurrency investments. The simplicity with which an asset can be purchased or sold without significantly altering its price is referred to as liquidity. Cryptocurrencies with higher liquidity tend to have more active markets, making it easier for investors to enter or exit positions. High liquidity can reduce the risk of encountering slippage, where the execution price of a trade differs from the expected price due to market volatility or order book depth. Additionally, liquid markets allow investors to react quickly to market trends and capitalize on profit opportunities.

Rapid technological advancements and innovations drive the cryptocurrency market. Projects are constantly being developed, and new cryptocurrencies are introduced regularly. Evaluating the technological merits of a cryptocurrency project is crucial in determining its capacity for long-term success. Investors should consider factors such as the underlying blockchain technology, the project's use case, its development team's credentials, and its community support. Projects with strong technological fundamentals and straightforward utility are more likely to sustain their value and attract continued interest from investors.

Diversification is a fundamental principle of investment strategy and applies to cryptocurrency investments. Due to the inherent volatility and uncertainties of the cryptocurrency market, investors should avoid putting all their funds into a single cryptocurrency. Diversifying across different cryptocurrencies and other asset classes can help spread risk and balance potential losses. Additionally, diversification allows investors to participate in multiple projects with varying degrees of risk and reward.

Assessing the long-term potential of cryptocurrencies is essential for investors seeking sustainable growth. While short-term price movements can be affected by market sentiment and speculation, long-term value is more closely tied to the utility and adoption of the underlying technology. Investors should research the real-world use cases and potential impact of the cryptocurrency projects they are considering. Projects that address genuine problems and have the potential to disrupt existing industries or build new markets may have a higher chance of long-term success.

Education and due diligence are critical components of evaluating the risks and rewards of cryptocurrency investments. The cryptocurrency market is dynamic and complex, and staying informed about market trends, technological developments, and regulatory changes is crucial. Investors should thoroughly research individual cryptocurrencies, exchanges, and investment platforms. Understanding the risks associated with specific assets and investment strategies can help investors make well-informed decisions and avoid pitfalls.

Lastly, psychological factors can significantly impact investment decisions in the cryptocurrency market. Fear of missing out (FOMO) and fear of loss (FOL) are common emotions that can lead to impulsive actions and irrational investment choices. Investors should remain disciplined and adhere to their investment strategy, avoiding making emotional decisions based on short-term market movements. Maintaining a long-term perspective and managing emotions can help investors remain focused on their investment goals and reduce the impact of market fluctuations.

Cryptocurrency investments offer a unique blend of risks and rewards. The market's highly volatile nature can result in significant gains or losses within short periods. Regulatory uncertainties and security risks add further complexity to the investment landscape. However, the potential for technological advancement, market liquidity, and long-term value create opportunities for savvy investors.

To navigate the risks and rewards of cryptocurrency investments successfully, investors should approach the market with a well-informed and balanced perspective. Understanding price volatility, regulatory developments, technological advancements, and the importance of diversification can empower investors to make informed decisions aligned with their risk tolerance and investment objectives. By conducting thorough research, exercising discipline, and staying informed, investors can position themselves to capitalize on the transformative potential of cryptocurrencies while managing associated risks responsibly.

Understanding market trends and analysis

Cryptocurrency investment has emerged as a prominent avenue for individuals seeking to participate in the decentralized financial revolution. Understanding market trends and analysis becomes crucial for making informed investment decisions as the cryptocurrency market continues to evolve. Market trends include price movements, trading volumes, market sentiment, and technological developments. This section will delve into the significance of market trends and analysis in cryptocurrency investing. By examining technical and fundamental analysis, market indicators, and sentiment analysis, investors can gain valuable insights to effectively navigate the dynamic and often volatile cryptocurrency market.

Technical analysis is a popular approach cryptocurrency traders and investors use to predict future price movements based on historical price data and market statistics. The basic principle of technical analysis is that past price patterns and trends can offer insights into future price behavior. Several tools and methods are employed in technical analysis, including chart patterns, support and resistance levels, moving averages, and oscillators.

Chart patterns, including head and shoulders, double tops, and flags, are graphical representations of price movements that can signal potential trend reversals or continuations. Identifying these patterns allows traders to make educated decisions about buying or selling cryptocurrencies.

On a price chart, levels of support or resistance are horizontal lines that represent points where the price often finds support (stops falling) or resistance (stops rising). Having a thorough understanding of these levels can help traders choose the best times for entering and exiting their trades.

Moving averages smooth out price data and identify trends over specific time frames. They can help traders determine the market's overall direction and the trend's strength.

The RSI (Relative Strength Index) and Moving Average Convergence Divergence (MACD) are two oscillators that are used to identify if the market is overbought or oversold. These markers can reveal information about potential trend reversals.

While technical analysis can offer valuable insights into price movements, it is essential to recognize that market sentiment and external factors can influence cryptocurrency prices. Therefore, technical analysis should be complemented with other forms of analysis to gain a comprehensive understanding of the market.

Fundamental analysis entails evaluating the intrinsic value of a cryptocurrency by considering factors such as its underlying technology, use case, development team, community support, and potential for adoption. Fundamental analysis seeks to evaluate the underlying strengths and shortcomings of a cryptocurrency project, in contrast to technical analysis, which is more concerned with price data.

Assessing a cryptocurrency project's technological components is essential to figuring out whether it has the capacity to succeed in the long run. Understanding the project's use case, scalability, security, and interoperability can provide insights into its practical utility and relevance in the broader blockchain ecosystem.

The development team's expertise and track record are also critical factors in assessing the viability of a cryptocurrency project. A competent and experienced team is more likely to deliver on their promises and navigate challenges effectively.

Community support and adoption play a significant role in the success of a cryptocurrency. A strong, engaged community can foster network growth, encourage innovation, and drive user adoption.

In addition to evaluating individual cryptocurrency projects, fundamental analysis also involves keeping track of industry trends, regulatory developments, and macroeconomic factors that can impact the overall cryptocurrency market.

Market indicators provide quantitative data and metrics that can aid investors in understanding the state of the cryptocurrency market. These indicators can range from simple metrics like trading volume and market capitalization to more sophisticated metrics like the Bitcoin Dominance Index and Fear & Greed Index.

Trading volume represents the total number of cryptocurrencies traded in a given time frame. High trading volume indicates active market participation and interest, while low trading volume may suggest a lack of interest or a market in consolidation.

Market capitalization refers to the total value of all cryptocurrencies combined. It provides a snapshot of the overall size and health of the cryptocurrency market.

The Bitcoin Dominance Index measures the percentage of total cryptocurrency market capitalization represented by Bitcoin. Changes in Bitcoin's dominance can indicate shifts in market sentiment and the potential for altcoin rallies.

The Fear & Greed Index gauges market sentiment by analyzing various data points, including price volatility, market momentum, and social media activity. Extreme fear or greed in the market can signal potential trend reversals.

Sentiment analysis involves gauging the emotional state of market participants based on social media activity, news coverage, and other qualitative data. Market sentiment can highly influence cryptocurrency markets, as fear, uncertainty, and hype can drive prices to extremes.

Monitoring social media platforms, forums, and news outlets can provide insights into how investors perceive specific cryptocurrencies or the market as a whole. Positive sentiment can increase buying activity, while negative sentiment may trigger selling pressure.

However, sentiment analysis has its limitations, as market sentiment can be subjective and easily influenced by rumors or misinformation. Therefore, it is essential to balance sentiment analysis with other forms of analysis to make well-informed investment decisions.

Understanding market trends and analysis is vital for successful cryptocurrency investing. Technical analysis helps investors identify price patterns and trends, while fundamental analysis assesses the underlying value of cryptocurrency projects. Market indicators provide quantitative data that reflects the market's overall health, while sentiment analysis gauges market participants' emotions and perceptions.

Investors can have a thorough grasp of the cryptocurrency market and make well-informed decisions that are in accordance with their goals for investing and risk tolerance by combining several forms of analysis. Additionally, staying informed about industry trends, regulatory developments, and technological advancements is essential for navigating the dynamic and rapidly evolving cryptocurrency market.

Cryptocurrency investing carries inherent risks due to the market's volatility and uncertainties. Therefore, investors should approach the market cautiously, conduct in-depth research, and seek professional advice when necessary. With a balanced approach to market trends and analysis, investors can capitalize on the opportunities the cryptocurrency market offers while managing potential risks responsibly.

Strategies for buying and selling cryptocurrencies

Buying and selling cryptocurrencies can be a complex and challenging endeavor due to the cryptocurrency market's highly volatile and fast-paced nature. As the market continues to evolve, understanding effective strategies for buying and selling cryptocurrencies becomes crucial for investors seeking to capitalize on opportunities and manage risks responsibly. This section will explore various strategies for buying and selling cryptocurrencies. From timing the market and setting entry and exit points to employing risk management techniques, these strategies can help investors navigate the dynamic cryptocurrency landscape and make informed investment decisions.

Timing the market is a strategy that entails identifying optimal entry and exit points based on market trends and price movements. While it may seem tempting to buy cryptocurrencies during periods of rapid price appreciation, doing so can expose investors to higher risks of buying at the peak of a price rally. Similarly, selling during price dips could lead to missed opportunities if the market subsequently rebounds.

As discussed earlier, investors often rely on technical analysis to time the market effectively. Investors can make more knowledgeable decisions about when to enter or exit positions by analyzing price charts and identifying support and resistance levels.

However, it is essential to recognize that market timing is inherently speculative and can be challenging to execute consistently. Instead of trying to time the market perfectly, some investors employ dollar-cost averaging (DCA). DCA involves regularly investing a fixed amount of money, regardless of the cryptocurrency's price. This strategy can help smooth out the impact of market volatility and reduce the risk associated with timing the market.

Setting entry and exit points is a risk management strategy that helps investors protect their capital and lock in profits. Establishing clear entry and exit criteria before trading can help investors avoid emotional decision-making and stick to their investment plan.

For example, when buying a cryptocurrency, an investor might set an entry point at a specific price level that aligns with their analysis and risk tolerance. If the price reaches that level, the investor will execute the purchase. On the other hand, setting an exit point involves determining a target price or price range at which the investor intends to sell the cryptocurrency to secure profits or limit losses.

Setting stop-loss orders is another crucial element of risk management. A stop-loss order is an instruction to sell a cryptocurrency once it reaches a particular price level. This strategy can help limit potential losses if the market moves against the investor's position.

Investors can adopt either a long-term or short-term approach to cryptocurrency investing, each with its own advantages and considerations.

Long-term investing involves holding onto cryptocurrencies for an extended period, typically several months to years. This strategy is often associated with a "buy and hold" mentality, where investors believe in the long-term potential of the cryptocurrency and are willing to weather short-term price fluctuations. Long-term investors seek to capitalize on the overall growth of the cryptocurrency market and the ability for significant returns over time.

On the other hand, short-term investing involves buying and selling cryptocurrencies over shorter time frames, often days or weeks. This approach aims to capitalize on short-term price movements and exploit market volatility. Short-term trading requires more active monitoring and technical analysis skills, as market conditions can change rapidly.

Both long-term and short-term strategies have their merits and risks. Long-term investing may provide investors more stability and less stress, but it requires patience and conviction in the chosen cryptocurrencies. Short-term trading offers the potential for quick profits but demands a higher level of skill, discipline, and time commitment.

Diversification is a fundamental principle of investment strategy, and it is equally relevant in cryptocurrencies. Diversifying one's cryptocurrency portfolio involves spreading investments across multiple cryptocurrencies and other asset classes.

The cryptocurrency market is known for its high volatility and uncertainties, making it susceptible to significant price fluctuations. Diversification can help mitigate the impact of adverse price movements on the overall portfolio. If one cryptocurrency underperforms, gains in other assets can help balance potential losses.

However, diversification should be approached thoughtfully, as investing in too many cryptocurrencies may dilute potential gains and expose investors to unnecessary risks. A well-diversified portfolio considers each chosen cryptocurrency's fundamentals, market trends, and risk profiles.

Thorough research and due diligence are paramount in the cryptocurrency market. With thousands of cryptocurrencies available, each with its unique features and use cases, investors must deeply understand the projects they invest in.

Research should involve assessing each cryptocurrency's technological fundamentals, development team, community support, market sentiment, and potential regulatory impact. Investors should also stay informed about industry trends, upcoming events, and partnerships that could influence the performance of specific cryptocurrencies.

Cryptocurrency markets can be influenced by news and social media sentiment. Investors should be cautious about reacting impulsively to market noise and instead focus on making decisions based on reliable and verified information.

Managing risk is essential in any investment strategy, and cryptocurrency investing is no exception. Cryptocurrencies are high-risk assets, and the market can experience extreme price fluctuations within short periods. Consequently, investors have to limit their investments to amounts they can afford to lose and steer clear of overexposure to the cryptocurrency market.

Diversification, as previously discussed, is a core element of risk management. Additionally, setting stop-loss orders and adhering to pre-established entry and exit points can help minimize losses and protect capital.

Investors should also be cautious about leveraging or borrowing funds to invest in cryptocurrencies, as it can amplify gains and losses. Leverage increases the level of risk and should only be used by experienced and risk-tolerant traders.

Strategies for buying and selling cryptocurrencies play a critical role in helping investors navigate the dynamic and highly volatile cryptocurrency market. Timing the market, setting entry and exit points, and employing risk management techniques are essential for successful cryptocurrency investing. Long-term and short-term investing approaches offer different opportunities and considerations, while diversification helps spread risk across various assets.

Thorough research and due diligence are paramount, as the vast and diverse cryptocurrency market. Staying informed about market trends, technological advancements, and regulatory developments can provide valuable insights for making informed investment decisions.

As with any investment, cryptocurrency investing carries inherent risks, and investors should approach the market with caution and responsibility. By adopting well-thought-out strategies and exercising discipline, investors can position themselves to capitalize on the opportunities offered by the cryptocurrency market while managing potential risks effectively.

Tips for managing a crypto portfolio

Managing a cryptocurrency portfolio requires a combination of prudent decision-making, risk management, and continuous monitoring. As the cryptocurrency market develops and matures, investors must develop effective strategies to navigate the dynamic and highly volatile landscape. This section will explore essential tips for managing a crypto portfolio. From setting clear investment goals and diversifying holdings to rebalancing and staying informed, these tips can help investors optimize their portfolios and achieve their financial objectives in the ever-expanding world of cryptocurrencies.

Before diving into the cryptocurrency market, investors should define clear and realistic investment goals. Establishing specific objectives, such as long-term wealth preservation, capital appreciation, or short-term profits, will guide portfolio management.

Different investment goals may require varying risk tolerance levels, investment horizons, and diversification strategies. Defining clear goals helps investors align their decision-making with their overall financial objectives, minimizing the influence of emotions and speculative impulses.

Diversification is a basic principle of portfolio management and is equally crucial in the cryptocurrency market. The cryptocurrency landscape is vast, with thousands of projects and tokens available. Diversifying across various cryptocurrencies can help spread risk and reduce the impact of adverse price movements.

Investors should consider diversification across different categories of cryptocurrencies, such as established cryptocurrencies like Bitcoin and Ethereum, promising altcoins, and potential growth-oriented projects. Diversifying into other asset classes, such as traditional stocks and bonds, can further enhance portfolio stability.

Managing risk is paramount in the highly volatile cryptocurrency market. Cryptocurrencies are known for their price fluctuations, and investments can experience rapid appreciation or substantial losses within short periods.

Setting stop-loss orders, which automatically initiate a sale if the price of a cryptocurrency falls below a predefined level, is a crucial risk management strategy. Stop-loss orders can aid in capital preservation and loss mitigation.

Another crucial component of risk management is only making investments that one can afford to lose. Cryptocurrencies carry inherent risks, and investors should avoid overextending themselves financially. Using only disposable income for cryptocurrency investments ensures investors can weather market downturns without jeopardizing their financial well-being.

Staying informed about the cryptocurrency market is vital for managing a portfolio effectively. The cryptocurrency space is dynamic, with continuous technological advancements, regulatory changes, and market trends shaping its trajectory.

Investors should actively seek reliable sources of information, such as reputable news outlets, industry publications, and authoritative cryptocurrency websites. Keeping abreast of market developments, project updates, and industry analysis can help investors make informed decisions and avoid reacting impulsively to market noise.

Continuous education is also essential, as the cryptocurrency market is complex and ever-evolving. Understanding the underlying technology, blockchain fundamentals, and various investment strategies can empower investors to navigate the market confidently.

As market conditions and cryptocurrency prices fluctuate, the composition of a portfolio can shift over time. Rebalancing involves periodically adjusting the allocation of assets to keep the desired risk and return profile.

Rebalancing can involve selling cryptocurrencies that have outperformed and reallocating funds to assets with greater growth potential. By regularly rebalancing the portfolio, investors ensure that their investments remain aligned with their long-term goals and risk tolerance.

It is essential to balance frequent rebalancing and allowing investments to ride out market cycles. Overtrading can lead to excessive transaction costs and may not always yield improved portfolio performance.

Emotions can be powerful drivers of investment decisions, and the cryptocurrency market is no exception. Fear of missing out (FOMO) and fear of loss (FOL) can lead to impulsive actions, such as buying at the peak of a price rally or panic-selling during a market downturn.

To avoid emotional decision-making, investors should stick to their pre-defined investment strategies and remain disciplined in their approach. FOMO and FOL often lead to chasing short-term gains or overreacting to market fluctuations, which can hinder long-term portfolio performance.

Maintaining a rational and disciplined approach, guided by clear investment goals and risk management techniques, can help investors overcome emotional biases and make decisions based on sound judgment.

Tax considerations are an essential aspect of managing a cryptocurrency portfolio. In many jurisdictions, cryptocurrencies are subject to taxation, and investors must be aware of the tax implications of their investment decisions.

Different types of cryptocurrency transactions, such as buying, selling, and exchanging between cryptocurrencies, can trigger taxable events. Keeping accurate records of all transactions and consulting with tax professionals can help investors ensure compliance with relevant tax laws and optimize their tax liabilities.

Managing a cryptocurrency portfolio requires knowledge, discipline, and continuous vigilance. Defining clear investment goals, diversifying holdings, and practicing risk management are fundamental principles for achieving success in the dynamic and volatile cryptocurrency market.

Staying informed about market trends, regulatory developments, and technological advancements empowers investors to make informed decisions and modify their strategies to changing market conditions. Rebalancing the portfolio periodically ensures that investments remain aligned with long-term objectives.

Emotional decision-making can harm portfolio performance, and investors should prioritize rationality and discipline in their investment approach. Finally, being mindful of tax considerations is crucial for optimizing tax liabilities and ensuring compliance with relevant tax laws.

As the cryptocurrency market evolves, investors must remain adaptable and continuously educate themselves to navigate the complexities and opportunities presented by digital assets. By employing these essential tips and maintaining a well-informed and disciplined approach, investors can maximize the potential of their cryptocurrency portfolios while managing risks responsibly.

CHAPTER IV

The Regulatory Landscape

Government regulations and their impact on cryptocurrencies

Cryptocurrencies have emerged as a disruptive force in the financial landscape, offering decentralized, borderless, and permissionless transactions. As the adoption of cryptocurrencies increases, governments worldwide are grappling with the need to regulate this new and evolving asset class. The regulatory landscape for cryptocurrencies is diverse, with different countries taking varying approaches to address issues such as investor protection, financial stability, money laundering, and tax evasion. In this section, we will explore the impact of government regulations on cryptocurrencies. From fostering legitimacy and institutional adoption to navigating challenges and preserving the core principles of decentralization, government regulations profoundly influence the cryptocurrency ecosystem.

Governments face the challenge of classifying cryptocurrencies within existing regulatory frameworks designed for traditional financial assets. Some countries categorize cryptocurrencies as commodities, while others consider them as currencies, securities, or property. The classification of cryptocurrencies can have significant implications for taxation, licensing, and reporting requirements.

The regulatory framework for cryptocurrencies may also depend on their specific use cases. For example, utility tokens, which provide access to a product or service, may be subject to different regulations than security tokens, representing ownership or financial interests in a project.

Clarity in regulatory classifications is essential for market participants and regulatory authorities to ensure compliance and provide a stable and transparent environment for cryptocurrency innovation and adoption.

Government regulations aim to strike a delicate balance between fostering innovation and protecting investors. On the other hand, regulations that promote investor protection can instill confidence and attract institutional investors, leading to increased liquidity and mainstream adoption.

Regulatory measures like Know Your Customer (KYC) and Anti-Money Laundering (AML) requirements can help prevent illegal activities, including money laundering and terrorist financing. Similarly, regulations that promote transparency and disclosure can aid in curbing fraudulent Initial Coin Offerings (ICOs) and unscrupulous practices in the cryptocurrency space.

On the other hand, overly stringent regulations can stifle innovation and hinder the development of new technologies. A balanced approach to regulation is essential to foster a supportive environment that encourages responsible innovation while safeguarding investors from potential risks.

The global nature of cryptocurrencies presents a challenge for governments seeking to implement consistent regulations. Each country has its unique financial and legal framework, leading to significant divergence in cryptocurrency regulations.

While some countries, like Malta and Switzerland, have embraced cryptocurrencies and blockchain technology, others have adopted more cautious and restrictive approaches. China, for example, has implemented strict bans on cryptocurrency trading and Initial Coin Offerings (ICOs), while countries like India and the United States have experienced periods of regulatory uncertainty.

The lack of global harmonization in regulations can create complexities for businesses operating in multiple jurisdictions and can impact cross-border transactions and investments. International cooperation and dialogue among governments are crucial to establishing common standards and promoting a globally inclusive regulatory framework.

Cryptocurrency startups and blockchain projects often face regulatory challenges and uncertainty. Obtaining necessary licenses, adhering to compliance requirements, and navigating complex legal landscapes can be daunting for startups, especially those with limited resources.

Regulations that offer clarity and guidance can create a conducive environment for startups to innovate and develop new blockchain-based solutions. Regulatory sandboxes, where startups can test their products and services in a controlled environment, have emerged as a popular approach to balance innovation and regulatory oversight.

However, overly restrictive regulations can lead to a flight of talent and innovation to more permissive jurisdictions, potentially stifling domestic innovation. Encouraging a flexible regulatory approach that fosters innovation while protecting consumers can promote the growth of cryptocurrency startups.

One of the basic principles of cryptocurrencies is decentralization, enabling peer-to-peer transactions without intermediaries. Some government regulations, particularly those aimed at combating money laundering and terrorism financing, may inadvertently compromise the privacy and anonymity of cryptocurrency users.

Regulations that mandate strict KYC and AML requirements on cryptocurrency exchanges and wallet providers can lead to the de-anonymization of users' transactions, raising concerns about privacy and data security. Balancing the need for user privacy with regulatory objectives is an ongoing challenge for governments.

Cryptocurrencies like Monero and Zcash, which prioritize privacy through advanced cryptographic techniques, may face increased scrutiny from regulators seeking to maintain transparency in financial transactions.

The rise of cryptocurrencies has also prompted central banks to explore the idea of Central Bank Digital Currencies (or CBDCs). These are digital versions of a country's fiat currency issued and managed by central bank.

Governments view CBDCs as a way to enhance financial inclusion, improve payment systems, and increase efficiency in monetary policy implementation. However, introducing CBDCs raises questions about the coexistence of government-backed digital currencies with decentralized cryptocurrencies.

CBDCs can have implications for financial stability, monetary policy, and privacy. The potential competition between CBDCs and decentralized cryptocurrencies has sparked debates about the future landscape of digital currencies and their respective roles in the global economy.

As cryptocurrencies gain popularity, businesses and financial institutions increasingly explore ways to integrate digital assets into their operations. However, the lack of regulatory clarity and compliance requirements can deter institutions from fully embracing cryptocurrencies.

Establishing clear regulatory frameworks can give businesses and institutions the confidence and legal certainty they need to participate in the cryptocurrency market. Regulated custodial services, institutional-grade trading platforms, and investment products can pave the way for broader institutional adoption of cryptocurrencies.

Government regulations profoundly impact the cryptocurrency ecosystem, shaping its development, adoption, and long-term viability. Striking a balance between fostering innovation, protecting investors, and preserving the core principles of decentralization is a complex and ongoing challenge for governments worldwide.

Clear regulatory frameworks that provide legal certainty and promote responsible innovation can create a supportive environment for cryptocurrency startups and blockchain projects. At the same time, excessive regulation that stifles innovation or compromises user privacy can hinder the growth of the cryptocurrency market.

International cooperation and dialogue among governments are essential to establishing global standards and harmonizing regulations in an increasingly interconnected world. By adopting a pragmatic and balanced approach to regulation, governments can harness the transformative potential of cryptocurrencies while safeguarding financial stability and investor protection.

Tax implications of cryptocurrency transactions

As cryptocurrencies gain popularity and become increasingly integrated into the global financial landscape, governments are grappling with the challenge of taxing these digital assets effectively. The unique nature of cryptocurrencies, such as their decentralization and borderless nature, presents complexities in determining the appropriate tax treatment for various cryptocurrency transactions. In this section, we will explore the tax implications of cryptocurrency transactions. From understanding how cryptocurrencies are taxed as assets or currencies to addressing issues of capital gains, reporting requirements, and tax evasion, a comprehensive understanding of cryptocurrency taxation is crucial for individual investors and businesses operating in the cryptocurrency market.

Classifying cryptocurrencies as assets or currencies can have significant implications for tax purposes. In some jurisdictions, cryptocurrencies are treated as capital assets or property, subjecting them to capital gains tax when sold or exchanged. This means that any profits realized from the sale of cryptocurrencies are subject to taxation based on the distiction between the purchase and sale prices.

On the other hand, treating cryptocurrencies as currencies may subject them to different tax treatment, such as income tax or value-added tax (VAT). In such cases, the taxation may vary depending on whether the cryptocurrency transaction is considered a personal use transaction or a business transaction.

Cryptocurrency classification can vary from country to country, leading to complexities for individuals and businesses operating across borders. Clarity and consistency in defining the tax status of cryptocurrencies are essential to promote compliance and avoid ambiguity.

Capital gains tax is a common form of taxation for many countries that treat cryptocurrencies as assets. When individuals or businesses sell or exchange cryptocurrencies for a profit, the realized gains are subject to capital gains tax. Capital gains tax can be short- or long-term, depending on the holding period of the cryptocurrency. Short-term capital gains are typically taxed at higher rates than long-term gains. The specific tax rates and holding periods vary from country to country. Cryptocurrency investors must maintain accurate records of their transactions, including purchase and sale prices, to accurately calculate and report capital gains.

Governments worldwide are increasingly focused on ensuring tax compliance in the cryptocurrency market. As a result, many countries have introduced reporting requirements for cryptocurrency transactions.

Cryptocurrency exchanges and other intermediaries are often required to report transaction information to tax authorities, similar to how traditional financial institutions report financial transactions. Individual investors and businesses involved in cryptocurrency transactions may also be required to report their transactions and holdings in their annual tax returns. Failure to follow with reporting requirements can result in penalties and legal consequences.

Cryptocurrency mining is the procedure of creating new coins and verifying transactions on a blockchain. Mining can be a taxable activity, depending on the jurisdiction and the specific nature of the mining operation. In some countries, mining activities may be subject to income tax or treated as a business activity, subject to business tax rates. The value of newly mined coins may also be considered taxable income. Understanding the tax implications of cryptocurrency mining is crucial for miners to comply with tax regulations and avoid potential liabilities.

Initial Coin Offerings (ICOs) are a fundraising method blockchain projects use to raise capital by issuing and selling new tokens or coins. The tax treatment of ICOs can vary depending on the jurisdiction and the classification of the tokens. In some cases, ICO proceeds may be subject to income tax, similar to traditional crowdfunding or fundraising activities. The tax treatment may also depend on whether the tokens are considered securities or utility tokens. As ICOs evolve, governments will likely introduce more precise guidelines for taxing token sales to provide certainty to market participants.

The borderless nature of cryptocurrencies can complicate tax implications, especially for cross-border transactions. Different countries may have conflicting tax rules and treatment of cryptocurrencies, leading to potential double taxation. Double taxation happens when the same income or transaction is subject to tax in two or more countries. Avoiding double taxation requires international cooperation and clear guidance on the taxation of cross-border cryptocurrency transactions. Tax treaties and agreements between nations can help mitigate double taxation and clarify the tax treatment of cryptocurrencies for international investors and businesses.

Cryptocurrencies' anonymous and decentralized nature can present challenges for tax authorities in enforcing tax compliance. Some individuals may attempt to evade taxes by using cryptocurrencies for transactions, especially in jurisdictions with limited cryptocurrency regulation. Some countries have implemented data-sharing agreements with cryptocurrency exchanges to combat tax evasion and increased scrutiny of cryptocurrency transactions. Tax authorities are also using blockchain analytics and forensic tools to trace cryptocurrency transactions and identify potential tax evasion.

The tax implications of cryptocurrency transactions are multifaceted and vary depending on the classification of cryptocurrencies, the type of transaction, and the jurisdiction. Governments worldwide increasingly recognize the importance of regulating and taxing cryptocurrencies to ensure compliance and protect their tax revenues.

Clear and consistent tax regulations that promote innovation and ensure tax compliance are crucial for fostering a healthy and sustainable cryptocurrency market. Individuals and businesses involved in cryptocurrency transactions must diligently understand and comply with tax obligations to avoid potential penalties and legal consequences.

As the cryptocurrency landscape continues to evolve, governments will need to adapt their tax policies to reflect the special characteristics of cryptocurrencies and the dynamic nature of the digital asset market. Effective taxation of cryptocurrencies can contribute to a more transparent and inclusive financial system, supporting the broader adoption of digital assets in the global economy.

A global perspective on crypto regulations

Cryptocurrencies have captured the attention of governments and policymakers worldwide, prompting diverse regulatory responses to this disruptive financial innovation. As the acceptance for cryptocurrencies continues to grow, governments face the challenge of balancing fostering innovation and protecting consumers and investors. The global perspective on crypto regulations is diverse, with countries taking various approaches, from embracing cryptocurrencies to imposing stringent restrictions. In this section, we will explore the global landscape of crypto regulations. From regulatory sandboxes and licensing requirements to addressing money laundering and ensuring financial stability, a comprehensive understanding of international crypto regulations is vital for both the cryptocurrency industry and governments seeking to harness the potential of this emerging asset class.

Crypto regulations vary significantly from one nation to another, reflecting the diverse legal, financial, and cultural landscapes. While some countries have embraced cryptocurrencies and blockchain technology, providing a conducive environment for innovation and investment, others have opted for stricter controls or outright bans. Countries like Japan and Switzerland have taken a progressive stance on crypto regulations, offering clarity and legal certainty to market participants. Japan, for instance, introduced a licensing regime for cryptocurrency exchanges and recognized Bitcoin as legal tender. Switzerland has established a regulatory framework that fosters innovation through regulatory sandboxes and a friendly approach to initial coin offerings (ICOs). Conversely, China and India have implemented more stringent regulations. China has banned cryptocurrency trading and ICOs, citing financial stability and investor protection concerns. India, too, has shown ambivalence towards cryptocurrencies, with regulatory uncertainty impacting the local crypto industry.

Regulatory sandboxes have emerged as a popular approach for governments to balance innovation and consumer protection. These sandboxes allow blockchain and crypto startups to test their goods and services in a controlled and supervised environment. Countries including the United Kingdom, Singapore, and Australia have embraced regulatory sandboxes to foster innovation and explore the potential applications of blockchain technology. By collaborating with startups, governments can gain valuable insights into the benefits and challenges of blockchain technology without compromising financial stability. Regulatory sandboxes also offer a platform for startups to engage with regulators, collaborate on solutions, and ensure compliance with evolving regulations.

Cryptocurrencies' pseudonymous and borderless nature has raised concerns about their potential misuse for illicit activities such as money laundering and terrorist financing. Governments are increasingly implementing measures to address these risks. Many countries have introduced Anti-Money Laundering (AML) and Know Your Customer (KYC) regulations for cryptocurrency exchanges and wallet providers. These regulations require these entities to verify the identities of their customers and report doubtful transactions to authorities. International cooperation is crucial to combating cross- border money laundering using cryptocurrencies. Organizations like Financial Action Task Force (FATF) is significant in setting global standards for AML and countering the financing of terrorism (or CFT) in the cryptocurrency sector.

As the cryptocurrency market expands, protecting consumers from fraud, scams, and unscrupulous practices becomes a priority for regulators. The decentralized nature of cryptocurrencies can make it challenging to hold bad actors accountable, necessitating robust regulatory oversight. Some countries have implemented consumer protection measures, such as requiring exchanges to maintain insurance or reserve funds to compensate customers in case of a breach or hack. Education and awareness campaigns are also essential to empower consumers to make knowledgeable decisions and avoid falling victim to fraudulent schemes.

The rapid development of the cryptocurrency market has raised concerns about its potential impact on financial stability. Governments are keen to ensure that the expansion of cryptocurrencies does not pose systemic risks to traditional financial systems. Financial regulators in some countries have taken measures to monitor and assess the probable risks of cryptocurrencies. These measures may include stress testing and scenario analyses to understand the implications of extreme market events. Central banks in some countries have explored the idea of Central Bank Digital Currencies as a potential tool for enhancing financial stability and improving the efficiency of payment systems.

Cryptocurrencies' tax treatment varies from country to country, reflecting different approaches to taxing digital assets. Some countries treat cryptocurrencies as assets subject to capital gains tax when sold or exchanged. Others may treat them as currencies, subjecting them to income tax or value-added tax (VAT) depending on the nature of the transaction. The borderless nature of cryptocurrencies can complicate tax implications for cross-border transactions, leading to potential double taxation challenges.

The internaional nature of cryptocurrencies presents challenges for regulators, as regulatory arbitrage and cross-border transactions can impact regulatory effectiveness. International cooperation and harmonization of regulations are crucial to address cross-border challenges and create a level playing field for market participants. However, achieving global consensus on crypto regulations remains a complex task, given different countries' divergent approaches and priorities.

The global perspective on crypto regulations is diverse and reflects the complexity of balancing innovation, consumer protection, and financial stability. As the cryptocurrency market continues to evolve, governments worldwide face the challenge of crafting appropriate regulations that foster innovation while safeguarding the interests of consumers and investors.

Regulatory sandboxes, AML measures, and consumer protection initiatives offer valuable tools to address the challenges posed by cryptocurrencies. Ensuring a transparent and inclusive regulatory environment can unlock the potential of cryptocurrencies and blockchain technology while mitigating the risks associated with their decentralized nature.

International cooperation and dialogue are essential to harmonize crypto regulations and prevent regulatory arbitrage. By learning from the experiences of different countries and adopting a pragmatic approach to regulation, governments can leverage the transformative potential of cryptocurrencies to build a more efficient, inclusive, and secure global financial system.

CHAPTER V

Security and Risks

Common security threats in the crypto space

The quick development of the cryptocurrency market has brought about significant technological advancements and opportunities for financial innovation. However, the crypto space also faces many security threats that can jeopardize digital assets' integrity, confidentiality, and availability. From hacking incidents and phishing attacks to Ponzi schemes and fraudulent Initial Coin Offerings (ICOs), the security landscape in the crypto space is complex and ever-evolving. This section will explore the common security threats in the crypto space. Understanding these threats is crucial for investors, businesses, and developers to implement robust security measures and safeguard against potential vulnerabilities.

Hacking and cyberattacks are among the most prevalent security threats in the crypto space. Cryptocurrency exchanges, wallets, and other platforms are attractive targets for cybercriminals due to the potential for stealing large sums of digital assets. Hackers use techniques such as phishing attacks, malware, and social engineering to compromise user accounts and gain unauthorized access to private keys or passwords. Once a hacker gains control of a user's assets, the funds can be irreversibly transferred to other accounts, making recovery challenging. In recent years, several high-profile hacking incidents have resulted in substantial losses for investors and businesses, highlighting the importance of robust cybersecurity measures.

Phishing attacks are deceptive techniques cybercriminals use to trick individuals into disclosing their sensitive information, such as login credentials or private keys. Phishing attacks often involve sending fraudulent emails, messages, or websites that mimic legitimate platforms or communications. Unsuspecting users may unknowingly provide their private keys or passwords to attackers, who then use this information to gain unauthorized access to their crypto wallets or accounts. Educating users about the risks of phishing attacks and adopting multi-factor authentication can help mitigate this threat.

The crypto space has witnessed a proliferation of Ponzi schemes and scams that promise high returns on investments but are, in reality, fraudulent schemes. These schemes often target inexperienced or unsuspecting investors, luring them with promises of quick profits. However, instead of generating legitimate returns, these schemes rely on funds from latest investors to pay returns to earlier investors, creating a pyramid-like structure. Regulators worldwide are increasingly cracking down on such fraudulent schemes to protect investors and maintain market integrity.

Initial Coin Offerings (ICOs) are fundraising events where blockchain projects issue and sell new tokens to raise capital. While ICOs have enabled many legitimate projects to secure funding, fraudulent ICOs have been a recurring issue in the crypto space. Fraudulent ICOs may promise revolutionary technology or exaggerated returns but eventually fail to deliver on their promises. Investors may end up losing their investments as these projects turn out to be scams. Investors should conduct thorough due diligence before participating in any ICO and be wary of projects that lack transparency or have unrealistic claims.

Smart contracts, self-executing contracts with predefined rules written on blockchain platforms like Ethereum, are prone to vulnerabilities that malicious actors can exploit. Errors or bugs in smart contract code can lead to unintended consequences, such as losing funds or access control issues. The infamous DAO (Decentralized Autonomous Organization) hack in 2016 is a notable example, where attackers exploited a weaknesses in the smart contract code to drain millions of dollars worth of Ether. Smart contract developers must conduct thorough testing and audits to identify and rectify potential vulnerabilities before deploying contracts.

Insider threats occur when individuals with access to sensitive information or systems misuse their privileges for malicious purposes. In the crypto space, insider threats can be particularly damaging, as those with access to private keys or sensitive data can embezzle funds or compromise security measures. Implementing strict access controls, regular monitoring, and background checks for employees and administrators can help mitigate insider threats.

Centralized cryptocurrency exchanges act as intermediaries between buyers and sellers, offering convenience and liquidity. However, these exchanges also present certain security risks. Since centralized exchanges control users' private keys, they become attractive targets for hackers seeking to access large pools of digital assets. Several high-profile exchange hacks have resulted in significant user losses and highlighted the importance of secure custody practices. Users may opt for decentralized exchanges or custodial solutions that employ multi-signature wallets or other secure storage methods to mitigate custodial risks.

The crypto space is not immune to security threats, and the evolving nature of these threats demands constant vigilance and proactive security measures. From hacking and phishing attacks to Ponzi schemes and smart contract vulnerabilities, the crypto ecosystem faces diverse security challenges. To protect against these threats, investors, businesses, and developers must prioritize cybersecurity and adopt best practices. User education, multi-factor authentication, secure storage solutions, and thorough smart contract audits are some measures that can help mitigate risks. Additionally, governments and regulators are crucial in maintaining market integrity and protecting investors from deceitful activities. By fostering a secure and transparent regulatory environment, regulators can promote responsible innovation and support the long-term growth and sustainability of the crypto space. Through collaboration between stakeholders and ongoing efforts to address emerging security threats, the crypto industry can continue to advance and realize its transformative potential in the global financial landscape.

Best practices for securing your cryptocurrencies

As cryptocurrencies gain popularity and acceptance, ensuring the security of digital assets has become paramount. Cryptocurrency transactions' decentralized and irreversible nature makes them attractive to legitimate users and malicious actors. Everyone involved in the crypto space from individual investors to businesses and institutions must adopt best practices to safeguard their cryptocurrencies from potential threats. In this section, we will explore the best practices for securing cryptocurrencies. From choosing secure wallets and employing strong passwords to implementing two- factor authentication and staying informed about the latest security trends, these practices can significantly enhance the protection of digital assets and instill confidence in the broader adoption of cryptocurrencies.

The first step in securing cryptocurrencies is selecting a secure and reputable wallet. Wallets are either software or hardware applications that allow users to keep, send, and receive cryptocurrencies. There are numerous types of wallets, including software wallets (online and offline) and hardware wallets. Hardware wallets, such as Ledger and Trezor, are considered one of the most secure options as they store private keys offline, reducing the risk of exposure to online threats. However, reputable software wallets with solid security features can also provide a safe storage solution. When choosing a wallet, it is essential to research the wallet provider, read user reviews, and ensure that it supports the cryptocurrencies you intend to store. Additionally, always download wallets from official sources to avoid the risk of downloading malware-infected versions.

Creating strong and unique passwords is fundamental in protecting cryptocurrencies. Avoid using simple passwords, such as "password123" or personal information like birthdates and names. Rather, build complex passwords using a mix of uppercase and lowercase letters, numbers, as well as special characters. Enabling two-factor authentication (2FA) adds an extra layer of security to your accounts. With 2FA, users must provide a second verification code, usually generated through an authenticator app or received via SMS, in addition to their password. This additional step makes it significantly harder for unauthorized individuals to access your accounts.

Cryptocurrency wallets and devices require regular updates to patch security vulnerabilities and bugs. Keeping the software and firmware updated is crucial to maintaining the highest level of security. Wallet providers often release updates to enhance security features, fix software bugs, and address emerging threats. Failing to update your wallet may expose your cryptocurrencies to potential risks, as attackers may exploit known vulnerabilities to gain unauthorized access. Always check for updates from the official sources of your wallets or devices and follow the recommended update procedures.

Backing up your cryptocurrency wallets is essential in case of hardware failure, loss, or theft. A backup allows you to recover your funds and access your cryptocurrencies from a new device if necessary. When creating a backup, storing it securely and offline is crucial. Avoid saving backups on cloud storage or sharing them online, as this can expose your private keys to potential risks. Consider using encrypted external storage devices or even writing down your seed phrase or private keys on paper and storing them in a physically secure location.

Multi-signature transactions, or multi-sig, require multiple private keys to authorize a transaction. This feature adds a further layer of security and prevents unauthorized access to funds even if one private key is compromised. For example, a multi-sig wallet may require two out of three private keys to authorize a transaction. If one key is jeopardized, the funds will stay secure as the attacker would need at least one more key to initiate a transaction.

Phishing attacks and scams are prevalent in the crypto space, and educating yourself about these tactics is crucial to avoid falling victim to them. Phishing attacks involve deceptive emails, websites, or messages designed to trick users into disclosing their private keys or login credentials. Always be cautious about clicking on suspicious links and verify the authenticity of the websites you visit. Additionally, be cautious of investment schemes that promise guaranteed high returns or pressure you to act quickly. If an offer seems too good to be true, it likely is.

Diversification is a risk management strategy that can protect your crypto portfolio from significant losses. Consider spreading your investments across multiple assets instead of putting all your funds into a single cryptocurrency. Diversification can help mitigate the influence of market volatility and mitigate the risk of losing all your funds due to a sudden drop in a single cryptocurrency's value.

Cold storage involves keeping cryptocurrencies offline, away from internet-connected devices. This method is particularly suitable for long-term holding and large sums of cryptocurrencies that you do not plan to trade frequently. Hardware wallets, paper wallets, or other forms of offline storage are commonly used for cold storage. Keeping your funds offline minimizes the risk of exposure to online threats, such as hacking and phishing attacks.

The cryptocurrency space is constantly evolving, and new security threats may emerge. Staying informed about the most current security trends and best practices is essential in maintaining the security of your cryptocurrencies. Regularly check for updates from reputable sources, follow security-related news and announcements, and participate in community forums to learn from other users' experiences.

Securing cryptocurrencies is a crucial responsibility for all individuals, businesses, and institutions involved in crypto. By implementing best practices such as choosing secure wallets, using strong passwords and two-factor authentication, keeping software and firmware up to date, and backing up wallets securely, users can significantly reduce the risk of potential threats. Additionally, staying informed about phishing and scams, diversifying your crypto portfolio, using cold storage for long-term holding, and remaining vigilant in the face of evolving security challenges can help protect digital assets from unauthorized access and potential losses. As the crypto space grows, proactive security measures and education will play a pivotal role in fostering confidence in cryptocurrencies and their broader adoption in the global financial landscape.

Recognizing and avoiding scams and frauds

The cryptocurrency market has witnessed exponential growth recently, attracting many investors seeking to capitalize on its potential. However, the crypto space is not immune to scams and frauds, and investors must exercise caution and due diligence to protect themselves from malicious actors. From Ponzi schemes and fake ICOs to pump-and-dump schemes and phishing attacks, the variety of scams and frauds in the crypto space is vast and ever-evolving. In this section, we will explore the various types of scams and frauds prevalent in the cryptocurrency market and provide actionable insights for investors to recognize and prevent falling victim to them. Educating oneself about the warning signs and adopting best practices can empower investors to make informed decisions and participate responsibly in the crypto market.

Ponzi schemes have long been associated with financial fraud, and the cryptocurrency market is no exception. In a typical Ponzi scheme, the perpetrator promises high returns on investment to early participants, funded by the contributions of new investors. These schemes collapse when there are not enough new investors to sustain the promised returns, leaving many investors with significant losses. Fake Initial Coin Offerings (ICOs) are another common form of cryptocurrency fraud. In a fake ICO, fraudsters create a website and a whitepaper for a non-existent project, enticing investors to buy no real value tokens. Once the fraudsters have collected enough funds, they disappear, leaving investors with worthless tokens. To avoid falling prey to Ponzi schemes and fake ICOs, investors should thoroughly research projects, scrutinize whitepapers, and verify the credibility of the teams behind them. Legitimate projects have transparent goals, detailed roadmaps, and active communities that engage with developers.

Pump-and-dump schemes entail artificially inflating the price of a low-value cryptocurrency through false or misleading information, creating a buying frenzy among unsuspecting investors. Once the price peaks, the perpetrators sell their holdings, causing the price to go down and leaving other investors with significant losses. Social media platforms, online forums, and messaging apps are common breeding grounds for pump-and-dump schemes. Investors should be cautious of overly optimistic claims and sudden price spikes, which can indicate a potential pump-and-dump scheme.

Phishing attacks are a popular form of cybercrime in the cryptocurrency space. In a phishing attack, fraudsters use deceptive messages, emails, or websites to deceive users to reveal their private keys or login credentials. Once the attackers have this information, they can gain unauthorized access to users' wallets and steal their cryptocurrencies. To avoid phishing attacks, investors should never click on suspicious links or provide sensitive information to unknown sources. Always verify websites' authenticity and double-check cryptocurrency platform URLs before entering login credentials.

Fake cryptocurrency exchanges and wallets are designed to mimic legitimate platforms, making it difficult for users to distinguish them from the real ones. These fraudulent platforms may look convincing but aim to steal users' funds or private keys. Investors should only download software and apps from official sources to avoid using fake exchanges or wallets. Verify the authenticity of platforms by checking for HTTPS in the website URL and conducting online research to read user reviews and feedback.

Some investors may fall victim to pump groups, where participants collaborate to increase the price of a particular cryptocurrency artificially. Members of these groups buy the cryptocurrency simultaneously, creating a temporary price surge, and then quickly sell their holdings to profit from the inflated price. This practice can lead to significant losses for those who join the pump late. Insider trading is another form of fraudulent activity, where individuals with privileged information about upcoming market-moving events exploit this knowledge for personal gain. To avoid getting involved in such schemes, investors should refrain from joining pump groups and refrain from acting on rumors or unverified information.

Fake airdrops and giveaways are common tactics used by scammers to lure users into revealing their private keys or sending cryptocurrencies to fraudulent addresses. These scams often promise free tokens or a chance to win significant amounts of cryptocurrency in exchange for sending a small amount of cryptocurrency as a registration fee. Legitimate airdrops and giveaways typically do not require users to send cryptocurrencies or reveal sensitive information. Investors should be cautious of any offers that seem too good to be true and verify the authenticity of such events before participating.

Perhaps the most effective defense against scams and frauds in the cryptocurrency market is education and staying informed. Investors should take the time to understand the fundamentals of cryptocurrencies, blockchain technology, and the risks involved in investing. Additionally, staying updated on the most current news and developments in the crypto space can help investors recognize potential scams or fraudulent activities. Joining reputable cryptocurrency communities and forums can provide valuable insights and protect against falling for false claims or unverified information.

The cryptocurrency market presents immense opportunities for investors, but it has risks. Recognizing and avoiding scams and frauds is essential for anyone involved in crypto. The variety of fraudulent activities is vast and ever-changing, from Ponzi schemes and fake

ICOs to phishing attacks and pump-and-dump schemes. To protect themselves, investors should exercise caution, conduct a profound research, and stay informed about the latest trends and best practices in the crypto space. By adopting these measures, investors can confidently navigate the crypto market, make informed decisions, and safeguard their investments against potential threats. As the crypto space continues to evolve, remaining vigilant and knowledgeable will be key to enjoying the benefits of this transformative technology while avoiding scams and fraudulent activities.

CHAPTER VI

Real-World Use Cases

How cryptocurrencies are used in everyday transactions

Cryptocurrencies have revolutionized the way we perceive and conduct financial transactions. From humble beginnings with the advent of Bitcoin, cryptocurrencies have now become a global phenomenon, with various digital assets being used in everyday transactions. As blockchain technology evolves, cryptocurrencies are finding their way into multiple industries and use cases, enabling individuals and businesses to transact securely, efficiently, and transparently. This section will explore how cryptocurrencies are used in everyday transactions. Cryptocurrencies have diversified their utility beyond traditional fiat currencies, from online shopping and peer-to-peer payments to remittances and charity donations. As the world embraces the digital revolution, cryptocurrencies are poised to play an increasingly notable role in shaping the future of everyday transactions.

One of the most common ways cryptocurrencies are used in everyday transactions is for online shopping and retail purchases. Numerous online retailers and e-commerce platforms have embraced cryptocurrencies as an alternative payment method. Major companies like Microsoft, Overstock, and Newegg accept Bitcoin as well as other cryptocurrencies for their products and services. This allows customers to pay for goods without relying solely on credit cards or traditional banking methods.

Online buyers find cryptocurrency to be a desirable option because transactions with them are usually quicker and have cheaper transaction fees compared with standard payment methods.

With the use of cryptocurrencies, peer-to-peer (P2P) payments are made easy and people may send money to each other without going through middlemen like banks. P2P transactions are beneficial for small-scale, informal, or international money transfers. Cryptocurrencies like Bitcoin and Litecoin allow users to send money to friends, family, or business partners across borders in a matter of minutes, regardless of the recipient's location. P2P payments through cryptocurrencies are especially beneficial for individuals in regions with insuffiecient access to banking services, as they provide a secure and cost-effective way to transfer funds.

Remittances, or money sent by migrant workers to their home countries, represent a significant portion of global financial transactions. Traditional remittance services often charge high fees and take several days to process transactions, causing inconvenience and financial strain for the senders and recipients. Cryptocurrencies have become an efficient remittance solution, reducing costs and transaction times. Using cryptocurrencies for remittances can be especially advantageous for individuals working abroad who want to send money to their families back home without incurring excessive fees.

Cryptocurrencies are increasingly being accepted in the travel and tourism industry. Some hotels, airlines, and travel agencies now allow customers to pay for their bookings using cryptocurrencies. Using digital assets will enable travelers to avoid foreign exchange fees and complications related to using credit cards in different countries. Additionally, tourists can carry cryptocurrencies on their digital wallets, providing a more secure and convenient payment method during their travels.

Cryptocurrencies have also found a place in charitable donations. Non-profit organizations and charities have started accepting cryptocurrencies to receive funds. Cryptocurrency donations can provide higher transparency, as donors can easily track how their funds are utilized on the blockchain. Moreover, accepting cryptocurrencies allows charities to reach a broader international donor base, eliminating geographical barriers and easing the process of receiving donations worldwide.

The gaming industry has embraced cryptocurrencies to transact in-game purchases and virtual goods. Some online games and platforms accept cryptocurrencies for in-game currency or to buy items, skins, or other virtual assets. Blockchain-based gaming platforms have also emerged, offering players actual ownership of their in-game assets, which can be purchased, sold, and traded outside the game environment.

The gig economy, characterized by freelance work and short-term contracts, has seen a surge in cryptocurrency usage. Cryptocurrencies provide an alternative to traditional payment methods for freelancers and gig workers collaborating with clients from different countries. By using cryptocurrencies, freelancers can receive payments instantly without complex banking processes, while clients can avoid high cross-border transaction fees.

Cryptocurrencies have started to find their way into real estate transactions, with some property developers and sellers accepting cryptocurrencies as payment. Using cryptocurrencies can offer a more efficient and secure payment method for high-value real estate deals. However, due diligence is crucial, as real estate transactions involving cryptocurrencies may present additional legal and regulatory considerations.

Cryptocurrencies themselves are increasingly becoming an investment option for individuals seeking to diversify their portfolios. Some investors buy and hold cryptocurrencies as long-term investments, hoping their value will appreciate over time. Additionally, cryptocurrency trading has become popular for individuals looking to profit from short-term price fluctuations. Cryptocurrency exchanges enable users to purchase, sell, and trade various digital assets, providing liquidity to the crypto market.

The use of cryptocurrencies in everyday transactions has grown significantly in recent years. Cryptocurrencies have diversified their utility beyond traditional fiat currencies, from online shopping and retail purchases to peer-to-peer payments, remittances, and charity donations. As blockchain technology continues to evolve, cryptocurrencies are finding applications in various industries and use cases, providing secure, efficient, and transparent means of conducting transactions. The adoption of cryptocurrencies in everyday life is still in its early stages, but the benefits they offer in terms of speed, cost, and accessibility are increasingly appealing to individuals and businesses. As the world embraces the digital revolution, cryptocurrencies are poised to play an increasingly notable role in shaping the future of everyday transactions.

The role of cryptocurrencies in remittances and cross- border payments

Remittances, the money transfer by migrant workers to their home countries, have been a crucial aspect of global financial transactions for decades. However, traditional remittance services are often associated with high fees, lengthy processing times, and limited accessibility, posing challenges for both senders and recipients. In recent years, cryptocurrencies have emerged as a transformative solution for remittances and cross-border payments, offering benefits such as speed, cost- effectiveness, and financial inclusion. This section explores the role of cryptocurrencies in remittances and cross-border payments. We will examine the challenges faced by traditional remittance systems, delve into the advantages of using cryptocurrencies for cross-border transactions, and discuss the potential impact of this technology on the future of global remittances.

Traditional remittance systems have long been plagued by several challenges that hinder the efficiency and accessibility of cross-border transactions. High transaction fees are a prominent concern, particularly for low-income migrant workers who often bear the brunt of these costs. In many cases, remittance fees can amount to a significant percentage of the total transfer, reducing the amount received by the recipient.

Another obstacle is the slow processing time for cross-border transactions. Funds can take several days or weeks to reach the intended recipient through traditional remittance channels. This delay can be particularly problematic when funds are needed urgently, such as for emergency medical expenses or essential living costs.

Furthermore, the accessibility of traditional remittance services is limited, especially in regions with inadequate banking infrastructure. Numerous individuals in developing countries lack access to formal financial services, making receiving remittances through conventional means challenging.

Cryptocurrencies offer a range of advantages that address the challenges posed by traditional remittance systems. First and foremost, using cryptocurrencies for remittances allows for significantly lower transaction fees compared to traditional banking methods. Since cryptocurrencies operate on decentralized networks, there are minimal intermediary costs, leading to cost savings for both senders and recipients.

Another significant advantage of cryptocurrencies is the speed of transactions. Blockchain technology enables near-instantaneous cross-border transfers, allowing recipients to receive funds within minutes rather than days. This speed is especially beneficial for individuals relying on remittances to cover essential expenses promptly.

Cryptocurrencies also offer a solution for financial inclusion, enabling individuals without access to formal banking services to participate in cross-border transactions. A digital wallet and internet access are all that are required to send or receive cryptocurrencies, making it a feasible choice for people living in underdeveloped areas.

Moreover, cryptocurrencies transcend national borders, providing a seamless and borderless way to transfer funds globally. Without the need for intermediaries such as banks, cryptocurrencies facilitate direct P2P transfers, removing the complexity and delays associated with traditional remittance networks.

As cryptocurrencies gain traction and public awareness increases, more remittance service providers and financial institutions are exploring their adoption in the remittance industry. Established companies like Western Union and MoneyGram have begun exploring blockchain technology to improve their remittance services, while some newer startups focus solely on offering cryptocurrency-based remittance solutions.

Additionally, partnerships between cryptocurrency platforms and existing remittance providers have emerged, enabling a bridge between traditional and digital finance. These collaborations aim to enhance the efficiency of cross-border payments and provide users with the benefits of both systems.

While cryptocurrencies offer promising advantages for remittances and cross-border payments, they also present some challenges and risks that require careful consideration. One primary concern is the volatility of cryptocurrency prices. The value of cryptocurrencies can experience substantial fluctuations within short periods, which may lead to a situation where the amount received by the recipient varies significantly from the time of the initial transfer. To address this issue, some platforms offer stablecoins, which are cryptocurrencies pegged to stable assets like fiat currencies, to mitigate price volatility during transactions.

Another challenge lies in regulatory compliance and anti-money laundering (AML) measures. Cryptocurrencies operate decentralized and pseudonymous, raising concerns about their potential use for illicit activities. Governments and financial institutions are actively developing regulations to address these concerns and ensure that cryptocurrency-based remittances comply with AML and know-your-customer (KYC) requirements.

Stablecoins, as mentioned earlier, play a critical role in enhancing the utility of cryptocurrencies for cross-border payments. These digital assets are designed to keep a stable value by pegging their worth to a specific fiat currency or commodity. As a result, stablecoins offer the benefits of cryptocurrencies, such as speed and cost-effectiveness, while also providing price stability and reduced exposure to market volatility.

Stablecoins have gained significant traction in the remittance industry because they offer a more predictable value during transactions. These assets provide a compelling proposition for both senders and recipients, as they minimize the impact of price fluctuations and provide a stable value for cross-border transfers.

One of the most significant advantages of cryptocurrencies in remittances is the potential to enhance financial inclusion for underserved populations. The inability of millions of people around the world to use conventional banking services prevents them from participating in the international monetary system. Without the need for a conventional bank account, one can use cryptocurrencies as an alternate means of taking part in international financial transactions.

For migrant workers and their families in regions with limited access to formal financial services, cryptocurrency-based remittance solutions can provide an efficient and accessible option to send and receive funds. Digital wallets can be created with minimal documentation, reducing the barriers for entry and making financial inclusion a reality for those previously excluded from the remittance ecosystem.

Blockchain technology, the fundamental technology behind cryptocurrencies, is crucial in transforming the remittance industry. Blockchain's distributed ledger allows for transparent and immutable record-keeping of all transactions. Every transaction is time-stamped and linked to previous transactions, ensuring a transparent and auditable trail of funds.

This transparency minmizes the risk of fraud and corruption in remittance transactions, enhancing security and trust in the system. Additionally, the decentralized nature of blockchain eliminates the need for intermediaries, streamlining the process of cross-border transactions and reducing costs.

Developing countries with insufficient access to traditional banking services can benefit significantly from cryptocurrency-based remittances. In regions with inadequate formal financial infrastructure, cryptocurrencies offer a viable alternative to receive remittances and participate in cross-border transactions.

Furthermore, the speed of cryptocurrency transactions can positively impact recipients' lives. Quick access to funds allows for prompt payment of bills, medical expenses, and other urgent needs. This can lead to enhanced financial stability and resilience for families relying on remittances as a primary source of income.

The widespread adoption of cryptocurrency remittances has the potential to impact global economies in several ways. For sending countries, reduced remittance fees translate to more money from migrant workers' families, contributing to increased consumer spending and economic growth.

Moreover, the cost-effectiveness of cryptocurrency remittances may incentivize more people to use formal channels for cross-border transactions. This shift from informal to formal remittance systems can lead to a more transparent and regulated remittance ecosystem, benefiting both senders and recipients.

In receiving countries, increased financial inclusion can lead to greater participation in the local economy, driving entrepreneurial activities and economic development. Access to affordable cross-border payment services can also promote financial literacy and empower individuals with greater control over their financial transactions.

Cryptocurrencies have emerged as a transformative solution for remittances and cross-border payments, addressing the challenges faced by traditional remittance systems. With lower transaction fees, faster processing times, and improved accessibility, cryptocurrencies offer a compelling alternative for individuals and businesses involved in cross-border transactions.

Stablecoins, in particular, play a significant role in enhancing the utility of cryptocurrencies for remittances by providing price stability and reduced exposure to market volatility. As the acceptance for cryptocurrencies and blockchain technology continues to grow, the impact on global remittances and financial inclusion will likely be substantial.

The potential benefits of cryptocurrency remittances are not limited to cost and efficiency; they extend to improving financial inclusion, driving economic growth, and empowering individuals with greater control over their financial transactions. However, challenges like the price volatility and regulatory compliance must be carefully addressed to realize the full potential of cryptocurrencies in the remittance industry.

As technology continues to evolve, governments, financial institutions, and remittance service providers need to collaborate and develop regulatory frameworks that ensure a secure, transparent, and inclusive remittance ecosystem. By leveraging the benefits of cryptocurrencies and blockchain technology, the world can move closer to a more efficient, accessible, and equitable system for cross-border transactions, benefiting millions of people around the globe.

Cryptocurrencies in the gaming industry and other applications

Cryptocurrencies have transcended their role as a financial asset and have found diverse applications in various industries. The gaming industry is one such domain that has witnessed significant integration of cryptocurrencies. Beyond gaming, digital currencies have permeated multiple sectors, enabling innovative solutions and transforming traditional processes. In this section, we explore the applications of cryptocurrencies in the gaming industry and other sectors. From in-game economies and virtual asset ownership to supply chain management and decentralized finance (DeFi), cryptocurrencies have demonstrated their versatility and potential to revolutionize numerous aspects of modern life.

Cryptocurrencies have ushered in a new era of in-game economies, enabling developers to design virtual currencies specific to their gaming ecosystems. These in-game cryptocurrencies, often called "utility tokens," can be used to purchase virtual goods, unlock exclusive content, or access premium features. Players earn these tokens through gameplay achievements or can buy them with real money, offering a seamless way to monetize gaming experiences.

Adopting in-game cryptocurrencies has further boosted the concept of play-to-earn gaming, where players can accumulate valuable digital assets with real-world value. Blockchain technology underpins these in-game economies, ensuring transparency and provable scarcity of virtual items, which enhances player trust and engagement.

Traditionally, players did not have actual ownership of in-game assets, as these items were held on centralized servers and could be revoked or deleted by game developers. Cryptocurrencies and blockchain technology have revolutionized this aspect, granting players genuine ownership of virtual assets.

Non-fungible tokens (NFTs) enable the representation of unique and indivisible digital assets on the blockchain. NFTs have empowered players to own and trade rare in-game items, such as skins, collectibles, and virtual real estate, without the risk of losing them due to centralized control. This newfound ownership has allowed players to capitalize on their digital possessions by trading, selling, or showcasing them in virtual galleries.

Cryptocurrencies have facilitated seamless cross-platform transactions in the gaming industry. Players can use digital currencies to purchase in-game assets across different gaming platforms, eradicating the need for multiple accounts and cumbersome currency conversions. Moreover, blockchain interoperability protocols enable cross-platform asset transfers, allowing players to utilize their virtual items in various games within the same ecosystem.

Supply chain management is a different sector that has embraced cryptocurrencies to enhance traceability and transparency. By integrating blockchain technology into supply chains, companies can create immutable records of every step in the production, transportation, and distribution processes. This transparent ledger enables stakeholders and consumers to verify the authenticity and origin of products, thus combating counterfeit goods and ensuring ethical sourcing.

Cryptocurrencies and smart contracts synergize to automate various processes in supply chain management. Smart contracts, self-executing agreements on the blockchain, facilitate the automatic execution of tasks once predefined conditions are met. This automation reduces human intervention, minimizes errors, and expedites transactions, thus streamlining the supply chain.

For instance, smart contracts can automate payment releases to suppliers upon successful delivery of goods, reducing payment delays and enhancing stakeholder trust. Additionally, smart contracts can be programmed to trigger alerts in case of any anomalies or disruptions in the supply chain, allowing for immediate corrective actions.

Cryptocurrencies have paved the way for decentralized lending and borrowing through DeFi protocols. DeFi platforms leverage blockchain technology and smart contracts to eliminate the need for intermediaries, allowing individuals to lend or borrow cryptocurrencies directly from one another.

These lending and borrowing services are permissionless, meaning anyone with a compatible wallet can participate in DeFi lending and earn interest on their holdings. Similarly, borrowers can obtain loans without credit checks or traditional collateral. This democratized financial system expands access to credit and interest-earning opportunities, particularly for individuals without conventional banking services.

DeFi protocols also enable liquidity provision through liquidity pools. Users can deposit their cryptocurrencies into these pools and earn rewards for offering liquidity to the platform. These pools support various cryptocurrency trading pairs, enhancing market liquidity and enabling decentralized trading.

Cryptocurrencies in DeFi have disrupted the traditional financial landscape, offering greater financial autonomy and democratizing financial services for individuals worldwide.

Real estate tokenization has emerged as a novel application of cryptocurrencies, making it possible to fractionalize real estate assets and represent ownership as digital tokens on the blockchain. Tokenized real estate allows investors to own a fraction of a property, making real estate investment more accessible and liquid.

These tokens can be exchanged on cryptocurrency exchanges, providing a secondary market for real estate investments. Moreover, tokenization offers advantages in terms of cost efficiency and increased liquidity, as investors can buy or sell fractions of a property without the need for traditional real estate transactions.

Cryptocurrencies facilitate international real estate transactions by bypassing the complexities and delays associated with traditional cross-border payments. Buyers and sellers can transact directly using cryptocurrencies, eliminating the need for currency conversions and international banking fees.

The role of cryptocurrencies in real estate is still developing, but the technology can potentially revolutionize the way properties are bought, sold, and invested globally.

Cryptocurrencies have introduced transparency and traceability to charitable donations. Non-profit organizations can receive donations in cryptocurrencies, and each transaction is recorded on the blockchain. This enables donors to track the utilization of their funds and ensures that donations are channeled to their intended purposes.

Cryptocurrencies have streamlined cross-border donations, allowing individuals worldwide to contribute to charitable causes without needing currency conversions or expensive wire transfers. This has expanded the donor base for non-profit organizations and made it easier for individuals to support causes they believe in.

Cryptocurrencies have transcended their initial role as financial assets and have found diverse applications across various industries. Cryptocurrencies have created in-game economies in the gaming industry, granted players true ownership of virtual assets, and facilitated cross-platform transactions. Beyond gaming, cryptocurrencies have impacted supply chain management by enhancing traceability and transparency, while smart contracts automate various processes. Cryptocurrencies have democratized lending, borrowing, and liquidity provision in decentralized finance through DeFi protocols. Moreover, cryptocurrencies have made their way into real estate through tokenization, offering fractional ownership and streamlined international transactions. In charitable donations, cryptocurrencies have increased transparency and made cross-border contributions more accessible. As the technology continues to evolve, the versatility of cryptocurrencies is likely to lead to even more groundbreaking applications in the future.

CHAPTER VII

The Future of Cryptocurrencies

Potential challenges and obstacles to mainstream adoption

The rise of cryptocurrencies has ignited significant interest and excitement among investors, technologists, and the general public. With the promise of decentralized financial systems, faster and cheaper transactions, and increased financial inclusion, cryptocurrencies have the potential to reshape the future of finance. However, despite their growing popularity, several challenges and obstacles hinder the mainstream adoption of cryptocurrencies. This section delves into the potential barriers cryptocurrencies face on their path to widespread acceptance and explores the necessary steps to overcome these challenges.

One of cryptocurrencies' most significant challenges is the lack of clear and consistent regulatory frameworks across different jurisdictions. Governments and regulatory bodies worldwide are still grappling with how to classify and regulate cryptocurrencies, leading to uncertainty for businesses and investors.

The absence of standardized regulations can deter institutional investors from entering the cryptocurrency market, as they are hesitant to invest in assets that may face sudden regulatory changes. Moreover, varying regulatory stances can create a fragmented and unpredictable landscape for cryptocurrency businesses, hindering their ability to operate and innovate effectively.

To encourage mainstream adoption, policymakers must work together to establish comprehensive and balanced regulatory frameworks that protect consumers, promote innovation, and foster market stability.

Cryptocurrency transactions and holdings are stored on decentralized networks and digital wallets, making them vulnerable to security breaches and cyberattacks. High-profile incidents, such as exchange hacks and fraudulent Initial Coin Offerings (ICOs), have raised concerns about the security and safety of cryptocurrency assets.

These security challenges can deter individuals from using cryptocurrencies for everyday transactions or long-term investments. A lack of understanding about safeguarding digital assets further exacerbates these concerns.

To address security issues, the cryptocurrency community must prioritize developing and adopting robust security measures. This includes promoting best practices for securing wallets and using hardware wallets for added protection. Additionally, exchanges and wallet providers must invest in advanced cybersecurity measures to safeguard user funds effectively.

Price volatility is a hallmark of the cryptocurrency market, with asset values often experiencing wild fluctuations within short periods. While this volatility can present opportunities for traders, it also deters many potential users who seek stable and predictable value storage.

The extreme price swings can lead to concerns about speculative bubbles, reducing confidence in cryptocurrencies as a dependable store of value or a exchange medium.

To overcome price volatility, cryptocurrencies need to mature as an asset class. As the market grows and liquidity improves, price fluctuations will likely stabilize. Adopting stablecoins, cryptocurrencies pegged to stable assets like fiat currencies, can also help mitigate volatility and foster greater confidence in the market.

As the popularity of cryptocurrencies grows, scalability issues have become more pronounced. For instance, the Bitcoin network's limited transaction throughput and slower processing times during peak periods can hinder its ability to handle large transaction volumes.

Scalability challenges can lead to higher transaction fees and longer confirmation times, making cryptocurrencies less practical for day-to-day transactions.

Cryptocurrency developers are continuously working on scaling solutions, such as layer-2 protocols and off-chain solutions, to address these challenges. As these technologies mature and are widely adopted, the scalability of cryptocurrencies is likely to improve, making them more suitable for mainstream use.

For the typical user, interacting with cryptocurrencies can be a challenging and daunting process. Managing private keys, navigating through various wallets and exchanges, and understanding the nuances of blockchain transactions can be overwhelming for newcomers.

The cryptocurrency industry must prioritize user-friendly interfaces and intuitive designs to drive mainstream adoption. Wallet providers and exchanges should simplify the onboarding process, streamline account management, and enhance customer support to make cryptocurrency usage more accessible to all.

Educational initiatives and resources can also play a vital role in improving user understanding and confidence in cryptocurrencies.

The perception of cryptocurrencies in the mainstream media and public opinion are significant in their adoption. While cryptocurrencies have made strides in shedding their association with illegal activities and dark markets, lingering concerns about their use in illicit transactions persist.

Additionally, high-profile scams and fraudulent schemes within the cryptocurrency space have eroded trust in the industry. To foster mainstream adoption, the cryptocurrency community must actively promote transparency, self-regulation, and compliance with legal and ethical standards.

Promoting responsible usage and educating the public about the potential benefits of cryptocurrencies can help change the negative perception and build trust in the technology.

The rise of cryptocurrencies represents a potential disruption to traditional financial systems and institutions. As a result, some legacy financial institutions and influential stakeholders may resist the adoption of cryptocurrencies, fearing the impact on their business models and regulatory frameworks.

The cryptocurrency community must engage in constructive dialogues with traditional financial institutions and regulatory authorities to address this resistance. Collaboration and partnership opportunities can help bridge the gap between traditional finance and cryptocurrencies, leading to increased acceptance and integration of digital assets into the global financial ecosystem.

The lack of interoperability between blockchain networks and cryptocurrencies can hinder seamless cross-chain transactions and data sharing. This fragmentation limits the efficiency and scalability of blockchain-based solutions, potentially slowing down mainstream adoption.

To overcome this challenge, the industry must work on interoperability protocols and cross-chain bridges that facilitate seamless communication between different blockchain networks. Increased interoperability will enable the development of comprehensive blockchain ecosystems that can effectively cater to various use cases.

Several challenges and obstacles mark the journey toward mainstream adoption of cryptocurrencies. Regulatory uncertainty, security concerns, price volatility, scalability issues, and a lack of user-friendly interfaces are some of the primary hurdles facing cryptocurrencies. Overcoming these challenges requires collaboration between the cryptocurrency community, governments, financial institutions, and other stakeholders.

By establishing clear and balanced regulatory frameworks, enhancing security measures, improving user experience, and addressing scalability concerns, cryptocurrencies can pave the way for widespread acceptance and integration into the global financial landscape. As these obstacles are discussed progressively, cryptocurrencies have the potential to revolutionize finance, empower individuals with greater financial autonomy, and foster inclusive financial systems that benefit people worldwide.

Emerging trends and technologies in the crypto space

Blockchain technology and cryptocurrencies are developing quickly, bringing in a new era of digital transformation and financial innovation. As the adoption of cryptocurrencies expands, the crypto space witnesses many emerging trends and cutting-edge technologies. This section explores some of the key trends and advancements shaping the crypto space's future. From decentralized finance (DeFi) and non-fungible tokens (NFTs) to layer-2 solutions and interoperability protocols, these developments drive the mainstream acceptance of cryptocurrencies and revolutionize various industries.

Decentralized Finance, or DeFi, has emerged as one of the most significant trends in the crypto space. DeFi is a collection of financial applications built on blockchain networks, offering services such as lending, borrowing, trading, and yield farming without intermediaries like banks or financial institutions. These services operate through smart contracts, automatically executing transactions based on predefined conditions.

DeFi platforms democratize access to financial products for individuals all over the world by enabling users to access financial services in a unrestricted and trustless manner. With billions of dollars locked in various DeFi protocols, this trend demonstrates the growing demand for decentralized and community-driven financial solutions.

Non-fungible tokens (NFTs) have taken the crypto space by storm, revolutionizing the concept of ownership and digital assets. NFTs represent unique and indivisible digital assets, such as artwork, collectibles, virtual real estate, and even ownership of physical items. Unlike cryptocurrencies, each NFT has its distinct value and cannot be exchanged one-to-one.

NFTs have unlocked new opportunities for creators, artists, and developers to monetize digital content and intellectual property. The trend has witnessed multimillion-dollar sales of NFT-based art, music, and virtual real estate, highlighting the immense potential of this technology to reshape the art and entertainment industries.

Blockchain networks' scalability and transaction speed have been a recurring challenge for cryptocurrencies. Layer-2 solutions are emerging as a promising response to this issue. Layer-2 protocols, like the Lightning Network for Bitcoin and the Polygon Network for Ethereum, operate on top of existing blockchain networks and enable faster and cheaper transactions.

These layer-2 solutions offload specific processing tasks from the main blockchain, alleviating congestion and reducing fees. As a result, users can enjoy a more seamless and cost-effective experience when using cryptocurrencies for everyday transactions and applications.

The proliferation of multiple blockchain networks has led to a lack of seamless communication between these platforms. Interoperability protocols address this challenge by enabling cross-chain communication and data transfer.

Protocols like Polkadot and Cosmos facilitate interoperability by allowing different blockchains to trade information and assets. This trend not only enhances the overall efficiency of blockchain networks but also enables the creation of comprehensive and interconnected blockchain ecosystems.

Central banks across the globe are actively exploring the development and execution of Central Bank Digital Currencies (or CBDCs). These are digital versions of fiat currencies issued and regulated by central authorities. Unlike cryptocurrencies, CBDCs are centralized and can function within existing financial systems.

CBDCs can reshape the traditional monetary system by offering increased transparency, efficiency, and financial inclusion. As governments and central banks move forward with CBDC trials and pilots, the landscape of global finance is set to undergo significant transformation.

Privacy and security have long been key concerns in the crypto space. In response, various projects and technologies are emerging to improve the privacy and confidentiality of blockchain transactions.

Zero-knowledge proofs, like zk-SNARKs and zk-STARKs, enable the verification of transactions without revealing the actual data, preserving user privacy. Additionally, advancements in secure multi-party computation and homomorphic encryption allow for confidential data processing on public blockchains.

These developments are crucial for addressing privacy concerns while ensuring the integrity and immutability of blockchain networks.

The environmental impact of blockchain networks, particularly proof-of-work (PoW) systems like Bitcoin, has garnered considerable attention. Emerging trends are focusing on building greener and more sustainable blockchains to reduce energy consumption and carbon footprints.

Proof-of-stake (or PoS) and delegated proof-of-stake (or DPoS) consensus mechanisms are gaining popularity due to their energy-efficient design. These protocols require validators to hold and lock up a certain amount of cryptocurrency as collateral, reducing the need for energy-intensive mining activities.

Additionally, projects are exploring integrating renewable energy sources to power blockchain networks, promoting sustainable practices in the crypto space.

Decentralized Autonomous Organizations (DAOs) are entities governed by smart contracts and operated by their community members. DAOs enable decentralized decision-making and governance, allowing participants to have a direct say in the development and management of the organization.

The rise of DAOs has unlocked new possibilities for decentralized governance, funding, and community-driven projects. DAOs are already being used to fund research initiatives, art projects, and open-source software development, showcasing their potential to transform traditional organizational structures.

The crypto space is experiencing a rapid evolution, with emerging trends and technologies transforming various facets of finance and industry. Decentralized Finance (DeFi) revolutionizes financial services, while Non-Fungible Tokens (NFTs) reshape ownership and digital assets. Layer-2 solutions and interoperability protocols address scalability and communication challenges, enabling seamless and efficient blockchain ecosystems.

Central Bank Digital Currencies (CBDCs) are redefining the concept of national currencies, while advancements in privacy and security technologies enhance the integrity of blockchain networks. Meanwhile, the quest for green and sustainable blockchains seeks to minimize the environmental impact of crypto mining.

The rise of Decentralized Autonomous Organizations (DAOs) heralds a new era of community-driven governance and collaboration.

As these trends continue to mature and evolve, they are set to drive mainstream adoption and revolutionize various industries, ultimately shaping a more decentralized, inclusive, and innovative global economy. Embracing these emerging technologies responsibly and collaboratively will be essential to harnessing their full potential and unlocking the promise of the crypto space.

The influence of central bank digital currencies (CBDCs)

Central Bank Digital Currencies (CBDCs) have emerged as a critical development in the world of finance, promising to reshape the future of money and payment systems. CBDCs are digital representations of a nation's fiat currency, issued and managed by central bank. As cryptocurrencies gain momentum, introducing CBDCs holds significant implications for the crypto space. This section explores the potential impact of CBDCs on the cryptocurrency ecosystem, addressing issues such as financial inclusion, monetary policy, privacy, and the relationship between CBDCs and existing cryptocurrencies.

One of the primary goals of CBDCs is to enhance financial inclusion by providing a digital form of money accessible to all citizens, including those without traditional banking services. CBDCs can leverage existing digital infrastructure, such as smartphones, to enable individuals to access financial services and make transactions more efficiently.

This move toward financial inclusion could also expand the user base of cryptocurrencies. As CBDCs become more widely adopted, individuals who were previously unbanked or underbanked may become more comfortable with digital currencies, paving the way for increased acceptance of cryptocurrencies as an alternative to traditional banking.

The introduction of CBDCs may have implications for commercial banks and their position in the financial system. With direct access to central bank digital currency, individuals and businesses may hold some of their funds in CBDCs rather than traditional bank accounts. This shift in behavior could impact commercial banks' deposits and lending practices.

Furthermore, CBDCs may increase competition between commercial banks and digital payment providers, including cryptocurrencies. As CBDCs offer a secure and efficient digital payment option, it may prompt individuals to explore alternative digital assets, including cryptocurrencies, for specific use cases with unique advantages.

The adoption of CBDCs raises privacy and surveillance concerns. Unlike traditional cash transactions, CBDC transactions are likely to be traceable, enabling authorities to monitor spending patterns and track financial activities more closely.

While central banks may implement privacy features in CBDCs to protect user data, concerns about exposing or misusing personal financial information remain. As a result, individuals seeking enhanced financial privacy may turn to privacy-focused cryptocurrencies that offer more robust anonymity features.

The emergence of CBDCs raises questions about the relationship between these state-backed digital currencies and existing cryptocurrencies like Bitcoin and Ethereum. CBDCs are centralized and backed by the government, whereas cryptocurrencies are decentralized and operate on public blockchains.

As CBDCs gain traction, some proponents argue that they may compete directly with cryptocurrencies as a medium of exchange and a store of value. On the other hand, others believe that CBDCs' centralized nature may drive individuals to seek the benefits of decentralized cryptocurrencies, such as limited supply and resistance to government control.

CBDCs can potentially revolutionize cross-border transactions by simplifying the process and reducing the costs associated with international transfers. With CBDCs, cross-border payments can become more efficient and almost instant, eliminating the need for intermediaries and reducing foreign exchange fees.

The impact of CBDCs on cross-border transactions may also extend to cryptocurrencies. As CBDCs streamline cross-border payments, they may facilitate greater use of cryptocurrencies in cross-border trade and remittances, offering additional advantages in speed and cost-effectiveness.

CBDCs present central banks with new tools to implement monetary policy and maintain financial stability. By issuing CBDCs, central banks can directly influence the money supply, interest rates, and economic activity. CBDCs could enable targeted and efficient monetary stimulus measures during economic downturns.

Introducing CBDCs may also affect the demand for traditional fiat currencies and impact currency exchange rates. As such, integrating CBDCs into the global financial system could influence the behavior of international investors, impacting cryptocurrency markets as well.

The development of CBDCs necessitates significant technological innovation, including the utilization of distributed ledger technology (DLT) and smart contracts. As central banks explore blockchain-based solutions for CBDC issuance and distribution, they contribute to the overall advancement of blockchain technology.

Additionally, CBDC projects may foster collaboration between central banks and the private sector, including blockchain and cryptocurrency industry players. This collaboration can lead to exchanging knowledge and expertise, further enhancing the adoption of blockchain-based solutions in various sectors.

CBDCs could play a role in combating illicit activities, including money laundering and terrorism financing. The traceability and transparency of CBDC transactions may enable authorities to track and investigate suspicious financial activities more effectively.

On the other hand, privacy-focused cryptocurrencies might continue to be viewed as a potential tool for illicit activities. As a result, regulatory scrutiny on privacy coins may increase, impacting their adoption and use in the crypto space.

The emergence of CBDCs marks a pivotal moment in the evolution of the financial system. While CBDCs offer the potential for enhanced financial inclusion, improved cross-border transactions, and technological innovation, they also raise concerns about privacy, monetary policy, and the relationship with existing cryptocurrencies.

CBDCs may complement the growth of the cryptocurrency ecosystem by introducing digital currencies to a broader audience and driving technological advancements. Simultaneously, they may also prompt individuals to explore the unique benefits of decentralized cryptocurrencies, fostering further adoption and innovation in the crypto space.

As central banks and governments continue to explore and implement CBDCs, it is essential to strike a balance between harnessing the advantages of digital currencies and addressing the challenges and risks that arise. Collaborative efforts between regulators, central banks, and the crypto industry will be crucial in shaping a sustainable and inclusive future for the global financial landscape.

CHAPTER VIII

Blockchain Beyond Cryptocurrencies

Understanding the broader applications of blockchain technology

Originally designed to power cryptocurrencies like Bitcoin, blockchain technology has evolved into a transformative force with far-reaching applications across various industries. Beyond its role in crypto, blockchain's decentralized, transparent, and secure nature has sparked interest and experimentation in numerous sectors. This section delves into the broader applications of blockchain technology, exploring how it revolutionizes finance, supply chain management, healthcare, identity verification, voting systems, and more. As blockchain matures, its potential to disrupt traditional systems and foster innovative solutions becomes increasingly evident.

The financial industry is one of blockchain technology's earliest adopters and beneficiaries. Blockchain enables the creation of decentralized finance (DeFi) platforms, which offer an array of financial services without intermediaries like banks. DeFi protocols provide lending, borrowing, and trading options with smart contracts, ensuring transparency and reducing counterparty risks.

Additionally, blockchain-based payment systems facilitate cross-border transactions with reduced fees and processing times. These innovations challenge traditional financial institutions and drive the evolution of the global financial landscape.

Blockchain technology is a revolutionary supply chain management by enhancing transparency and traceability throughout the supply chain. By recording every supply chain step on an immutable ledger, blockchain enables real-time monitoring and verification of product movements, ensuring authenticity and combating counterfeiting.

This increased transparency benefits consumers, businesses, and regulatory bodies, enabling greater visibility into product origins, quality, and compliance. Blockchain implementations in supply chains also streamline operations, reducing paperwork and delays, and improving overall efficiency.

The healthcare industry stands to acquire significantly from blockchain's capabilities. Medical records stored on blockchain are secure, interoperable, and accessible to authorized parties, streamlining patient care and medical research. Additionally, blockchain's data integrity ensures the accuracy and privacy of sensitive patient information.

Blockchain-based pharmaceutical supply chain solutions enhance drug tracking, combat counterfeit medications, and improve drug safety. The technology also enables efficient management of clinical trials and the secure sharing of medical data across institutions for research purposes.

Blockchain's potential to revolutionize identity verification lies in its ability to create self-sovereign identity systems. In these systems, individuals can control their digital identities and share only the necessary information with service providers.

Decentralized identity solutions reduce data breaches, as sensitive data is not stored in a central database susceptible to hacking. Instead, identity-related information is encrypted and distributed across the blockchain network, ensuring enhanced security and privacy.

Blockchain technology offers a robust foundation for secure and transparent voting systems. Blockchain-based voting ensures tamper-proof and auditable records, eliminating voter fraud or manipulation concerns. By enhancing voter confidence and participation, blockchain can strengthen democratic processes.

Smart contracts can automate voting procedures, ensuring accuracy and efficiency. Additionally, blockchain-enabled voting systems enable instant results, eliminating the need for labor-intensive counting and manual verification.

Blockchain technology is driving the emergence of Web 3.0, a decentralized internet where users have greater control over their data and digital interactions. Through blockchain-based platforms, users can browse the internet privately, free from invasive data tracking and advertisements.

Decentralized storage solutions, powered by blockchain, enable individuals to store data in a distributed network rather than relying on centralized servers. This technology mitigates the risk of data loss and hacking while enhancing user privacy.

Blockchain can revolutionize the way intellectual property rights are managed and enforced. Smart contracts can be utilized to automatically record ownership and license agreements for creative works, such as music, art, and written content.

This blockchain-based system streamlines the process of verifying originality and ownership, reducing disputes and ensuring creators receive fair compensation for their work. Additionally, it offers a transparent and accessible record of intellectual property rights, simplifying licensing and usage permissions.

Blockchain technology plays a crucial role in promoting energy efficiency and sustainability. Individuals can trade excess energy with others peer-to-peer by employing blockchain in energy management systems.

Blockchain-based energy platforms enable renewable energy producers to tokenize their production, attracting investment and encouraging the growth of green energy solutions. This innovation empowers consumers to choose sustainable energy options while contributing to a greener future.

The wider applications of blockchain technology span across many industries, revolutionizing established practices and opening the door to creative solutions. Digital age benefits greatly from blockchain's decentralized, transparent, and secure characteristics, which extends beyond voting systems and healthcare to include supply chain management and banking.

As blockchain evolves and matures, its potential for widespread disruption and positive impact becomes increasingly apparent. With the growing interest and investment in blockchain research and development, we expect to witness further breakthroughs and transformative solutions that will shape a more decentralized, transparent, and efficient world. Embracing blockchain's potential responsibly and collaboratively will be essential to realizing its benefits and overcoming potential challenges on the path to a decentralized future.

Blockchain in supply chain management, healthcare, and more

Blockchain technology's unique attributes, including decentralization, transparency, and immutability, have led to its widespread adoption across diverse industries. This section explores the transformative impact of blockchain in supply chain management, healthcare, and other sectors. By addressing trust, data security, and efficiency issues, blockchain is revolutionizing traditional systems and fostering innovation across various domains. From enhancing transparency in supply chains to streamlining patient care in healthcare, the applications of blockchain technology are reshaping industries and paving the way for a more decentralized and efficient future.

Supply chain management is an intricate process involving multiple parties, transactions, and information flows. The lack of transparency and traceability in traditional supply chains often results in inefficiencies, delays, and counterfeiting. Blockchain technology solves these challenges by creating an immutable and auditable record of every transaction and movement within the supply chain.

With blockchain, each participant in the supply chain, from raw material suppliers to end-consumers, can access a single, shared ledger. This shared visibility enables real-time tracking of goods, authenticity verification, and logistics optimization. By reducing intermediaries and enhancing transparency, blockchain improves supply chain efficiency, reduces costs, and bolsters consumer trust in the products they purchase.

In healthcare, blockchain's secure and decentralized nature holds immense promise in revolutionizing data management and patient care. Electronic health records (EHRs) are prone to data breaches and interoperability challenges, impacting patient privacy and healthcare outcomes.

Blockchain-based electronic health records empower patients with control over their health data while ensuring that sensitive information remains encrypted and accessible only to authorized parties. This decentralized approach to health data management enhances data security, streamlines medical research, and promotes collaboration among healthcare providers.

Moreover, blockchain's traceability capabilities are critical in drug supply chain management. The industry can combat counterfeit medications by recording every step of the pharmaceutical supply chain on the blockchain, ensuring patients receive authentic and safe drugs.

Identity verification is crucial in many sectors, including finance, healthcare, and government services. Traditional identity verification methods often involve cumbersome and time-consuming processes, increasing the risk of identity theft and fraud.

Blockchain-based self-sovereign identity solutions offer a revolutionary approach to identity verification. With self-sovereign identities, individuals maintain control over their personal information and selectively share it with trusted parties. By eliminating the need for centralized databases and intermediaries, blockchain ensures the security and privacy of identity information, reducing the risk of data breaches.

The integrity of voting systems is a cornerstone of democratic societies. However, traditional voting methods face challenges related to voter fraud and mistrust in the election process. Blockchain technology can address these concerns by providing secure and tamper-proof voting systems.

Blockchain-based voting solutions enable transparent and auditable elections. Each vote is recorded as a digital transaction on the blockchain, ensuring accuracy and immutability. By enhancing the security and efficiency of voting, blockchain fosters increased voter participation and trust in democratic processes.

Protecting and managing intellectual property rights are critical for creators and innovators across various industries. Traditional copyright and patent systems can be slow and expensive, hindering the ability to effectively enforce and monetize intellectual property rights.

Blockchain-based solutions enable the secure and transparent recording of ownership and license agreements for creative works and inventions. Smart contracts automatically enforce the terms of agreements, ensuring that creators receive reasonable compensation for their work and reducing disputes over intellectual property rights.

The real estate industry faces challenges related to property title verification, fraud, and cumbersome legal processes. Blockchain technology presents a potential solution to these issues by providing an immutable and transparent record of property ownership.

By storing property titles on the blockchain, the industry can streamline the transfer of ownership, reduce paperwork, and enhance the overall efficiency of real estate transactions. Smart contracts can automate the execution of sale agreements, removing the need for intermediaries and reducing transaction costs.

The energy sector is increasingly exploring blockchain's potential to revolutionize energy management. Blockchain-based energy platforms allow peer-to-peer energy trading, enabling individuals and businesses to purchase and sell excess energy directly from each other.

Decentralized energy systems promote renewable energy adoption by incentivizing producers to tokenize their production. This enables consumers to choose green energy options, contributing to an environmentally friendly and more sustainable energy ecosystem.

Blockchain technology's transformative impact extends far beyond its origin in cryptocurrency. By providing decentralized, transparent, and secure solutions, blockchain has found applications in supply chain management, healthcare, identity verification, voting systems, intellectual property, real estate, and energy management.

In supply chain management, blockchain ensures transparency and traceability, reducing inefficiencies and combating counterfeit goods. In healthcare, blockchain enhances data security, streamlines patient care, and strengthens pharmaceutical supply chains.

The self-sovereign identity solutions built on blockchain protect individual data privacy and streamline identity verification across sectors. In voting systems, blockchain fosters transparent and tamper-proof elections, promoting democratic integrity.

Blockchain revolutionizes intellectual property rights management, enabling creators to efficiently protect and monetize their works. In real estate, blockchain simplifies property title verification and transaction processes. Finally, blockchain's applications in energy management drive the adoption of renewable energy sources and promote sustainable practices.

As blockchain technology evolves and gain widespread acceptance, its potential to reshape industries and pave the way for a decentralized and efficient future becomes increasingly evident. Collaborative efforts between technology developers, businesses, and regulatory bodies will be vital in realizing the full potential of blockchain applications and ensuring its responsible integration into various sectors.

The concept of decentralized finance (DeFi)

Decentralized Finance, often called DeFi, is a groundbreaking movement that leverages blockchain technology to create an open and permissionless financial ecosystem. DeFi eliminates intermediaries like banks and traditional financial institutions, allowing users to access a wide range of financial services directly on the blockchain. This section explores the concept of DeFi, its core principles, and its revolutionary potential for reshaping the traditional financial landscape. From lending and borrowing to trading, asset management, and yield farming, DeFi challenges the status quo and empowers individuals with greater control over their finances.

At the core of DeFi lies a set of fundamental principles that differentiate it from traditional finance. Firstly, DeFi operates on blockchain networks, primarily Ethereum, creating a transparent and immutable ledger of financial transactions and operations. This transparency ensures that anyone can audit and verify every DeFi activity, promoting trust and accountability.

Secondly, DeFi is open and permissionless, meaning anyone with a connection in the internet can access and participate in DeFi protocols without requiring approval from central authorities. This inclusivity enables global financial participation, even for the unbanked and underbanked populations.

Lastly, DeFi employs smart contracts, self-executing code on the blockchain, to automate financial agreements and eliminate the need for intermediaries. Smart contracts ensure transactions are executed based on predefined conditions, reducing human error and enhancing security.

One of the primary use cases of DeFi is lending and borrowing. DeFi lending platforms enable users to lend their digital assets and earn interest, while borrowers can access funds by offering collateral. These transactions are facilitated by smart contracts, ensuring that borrowers can only access funds if they provide sufficient collateral to secure the loan.

DeFi lending protocols provide users with greater flexibility than traditional banking, as they can access loans without needing credit checks or lengthy approval processes. This approach to lending fosters financial inclusion and empowers individuals with access to capital.

Decentralized exchanges, or DEXs, are another crucial component of the DeFi ecosystem. Unlike centralized exchanges that use intermediaries to facilitate trades, DEXs operate directly on the blockchain. Users retain control of their funds throughout trading, eliminating the need to deposit funds on an exchange.

DEXs offer increased security and privacy, as users do not need to disclose their identities or personal information to trade. Additionally, DEXs provide users with access to a broader range of assets, including tokens that might not be listed on traditional exchanges.

DeFi also enables users to participate in asset management and yield farming. Yield farming involves staking or lending assets to liquidity pools in DeFi protocols, earning rewards through additional tokens. Users can compound their rewards by reinvesting them in other protocols, maximizing their returns.

Asset management in DeFi allows users to invest in various portfolios of digital assets, managed by smart contracts. This approach to investing provides users with greater control and transparency over their investments than traditional investment vehicles.

While DeFi presents numerous opportunities, it also faces challenges and risks. The openness and permissionless nature of DeFi can attract bad actors and expose users to potential scams and frauds. Smart contract vulnerabilities can lead to significant financial losses if not thoroughly audited and tested.

The lack of regulation in the DeFi space raises concerns about user protection and financial stability. Regulatory frameworks are still evolving, and the absence of oversight could potentially hinder the widespread adoption of DeFi.

Additionally, scalability and high transaction fees on blockchain networks like Ethereum can limit DeFi's accessibility and usability during periods of network congestion.

To address the challenges and risks in DeFi, the community is actively exploring innovative solutions. Auditing and security practices are improving to ensure smart contract robustness. Layer-2 solutions and cross-chain interoperability are being developed to enhance scalability and reduce transaction fees.

Moreover, the DeFi community is increasingly engaging with regulators to establish a framework that balances innovation with consumer protection and financial stability. Collaboration between traditional finance and DeFi is also gaining momentum, as bridging the two ecosystems can unlock new opportunities and drive mainstream adoption.

The future of DeFi is full of possibilities and potential disruptions. As blockchain technology matures and scalability improves, DeFi will likely become more accessible, efficient, and inclusive. DeFi could disrupt traditional financial systems by providing cost-effective and user-centric alternatives.

Cross-border finance may experience a radical transformation as DeFi enables seamless global transactions without intermediaries. Additionally, integrating real-world assets into DeFi protocols, known as decentralized asset tokenization, could unlock trillions of dollars of untapped value.

Decentralized Finance (DeFi) is a transformative movement that harnesses the power of blockchain technology to democratize financial services and challenge traditional financial institutions. By embracing transparency, openness, and self-executing smart contracts, DeFi gives users greater control over their finances and access to various financial services.

From lending and borrowing to decentralized exchanges, asset management, and yield farming, DeFi is redefining financial interactions and empowering individuals worldwide. Although DeFi faces challenges, innovative solutions and collaborations with regulators and traditional finance promise to pave the way for a more inclusive, efficient, and decentralized financial future. As DeFi continues to evolve, its potential to reshape global finance and foster financial inclusion remains at the forefront of the blockchain revolution.

CONCLUSION

Recap of key points covered in the book

Throughout this book, "Decoding Cryptocurrency: Navigating the Crypto Space - An Introduction to Virtual Money and Blockchain Technology," we embarked on a journey to explore the world of cryptocurrencies and blockchain technology. We delved into the foundational concepts, historical background, key characteristics, benefits, and various types of cryptocurrencies. We also examined how cryptocurrencies differ from traditional fiat currencies and explored the fundamentals of blockchain technology, mining, consensus mechanisms, wallets, and transactions. Additionally, we covered important aspects such as evaluating risks and rewards, understanding market trends, and developing strategies for investing and managing crypto portfolios. The book also shed light on government regulations, tax implications, security threats, and scams in the crypto space. Furthermore, we explored the broad applications of blockchain technology, including its impact on supply chain management, healthcare, voting systems, identity verification, and more. This section serves as a comprehensive recap of the key points covered in the book, bringing together the diverse facets of cryptocurrencies and blockchain technology.

Understanding Cryptocurrencies:

At the heart of our exploration was the fundamental understanding of cryptocurrencies as digital or virtual currencies that leverage cryptographic techniques for secure transactions. We discovered that the decentralized nature of cryptocurrencies enables peer-to-peer transactions without intermediaries. As the first cryptocurrency to appear in 2009, Bitcoin sparked a financial revolution that gave rise to thousands of additional cryptocurrencies with a wide range of features and applications.

Historical Background and Origins of Bitcoin:

We traced the origins of Bitcoin to an anonymous person or group known as Satoshi Nakamoto. The groundbreaking Bitcoin whitepaper laid the foundation for a trustless and decentralized digital currency. Over the years, Bitcoin gained widespread adoption, attracting enthusiasts, investors, and critics alike. Its success inspired the creation of alternative cryptocurrencies, each aiming to address specific issues or serve niche markets.

Key Characteristics and Benefits of Cryptocurrencies:

We explored the key characteristics that set cryptocurrencies apart from traditional currencies. The immutability and transparency of blockchain technology contribute to trust and security. Cryptocurrencies offer borderless transactions, lower fees, and faster settlement times, making them appealing for cross-border transfers and remittances. Additionally, we discussed how cryptocurrencies act as a store of value and a hedge against inflation, especially in times of economic uncertainty.

Different Types of Cryptocurrencies:

We dived into the diverse landscape of cryptocurrencies, examining the functionalities and unique features of prominent cryptocurrencies like Bitcoin, Ethereum, Ripple, Litecoin, and more. Each cryptocurrency serves specific use cases, ranging from digital gold to smart contract platforms, fast and low-cost transactions, and even privacy-focused transactions.

How Cryptocurrencies Differ from Traditional Fiat Currencies:

To understand the revolutionary impact of cryptocurrencies, we compared them to traditional fiat currencies. Unlike fiat currencies, that are issued and governed by governments and central banks, cryptocurrencies work on decentralized networks, free from governmental control. This difference has significant implications for financial privacy, economic stability, and the role of intermediaries in financial transactions.

The Fundamentals of Blockchain Technology:

To comprehend the underlying technology powering cryptocurrencies, we explored blockchain, a distributed and immutable ledger that records all transactions transparently and securely. Blockchain operates on a network of nodes, ensuring consensus and preventing data manipulation. We examined the proof-of-work and proof-of-stake consensus mechanisms that validate transactions and secure the blockchain.

Cryptocurrency Mining and Consensus Mechanisms: An

essential step in cryptocurrency networks is mining, which entails approving transactions, entering them onto the blockchain, and creating new coins as payment. We delved into the energy-intensive mining process and the rise of alternative consensus mechanisms like proof-of-stake, which offer energy efficiency and environmental sustainability.

Wallets and Private Keys:

As we explored the practical aspects of cryptocurrency ownership, we discussed wallets, which are digital tools used to store, send, and receive cryptocurrencies. Wallets can be hot or cold, with varying degrees of security and accessibility. Private keys, the cryptographic keys that grant ownership and control of cryptocurrencies, are crucial for safeguarding digital assets.

Transactions and the Role of Public Ledgers:

Understanding the process of cryptocurrency transactions, we explored how public ledgers record and verify all transactions on the blockchain. We covered the structure of transactions, transaction fees, and how miners or validators confirm transactions to ensure their inclusion in the blockchain.

Evaluating the Risks and Rewards of Cryptocurrency Investments:

We delved into the intricacies of cryptocurrency investments, emphasizing the importance of conducting thorough research, understanding risk factors, and avoiding common pitfalls. Cryptocurrency investments have risks such as price volatility, regulatory uncertainties, and security threats. However, they also present opportunities for substantial returns and diversification in investment portfolios.

Understanding Market Trends and Analysis in Investing in Cryptocurrencies:

We explored market analysis and technical indicators as essential tools for making informed investment decisions in cryptocurrency. Market trends, trading volumes, and sentiment analysis provide valuable insights into market behavior, aiding traders and investors in understanding price movements and potential opportunities.
Strategies for Buying and Selling Cryptocurrencies:

We discussed various strategies for buying and selling cryptocurrencies, including dollar-cost averaging, swing trading, and long-term holding. Each strategy caters to different risk profiles and investment objectives. We emphasized the significance of setting clear investment goals and developing a disciplined approach to navigate the volatile crypto market.

Tips for Managing a Crypto Portfolio:

Managing a crypto portfolio requires careful planning and risk management. We provided practical tips for diversifying a portfolio, managing exposure to high-risk assets, and avoiding emotional decision-making. Implementing these strategies can help mitigate risks and improve overall portfolio performance.

Government Regulations and Their Impact on Cryptocurrencies:

We explored the evolving regulatory landscape of cryptocurrencies as governments and financial institutions grapple with the implications of digital currencies. Regulatory actions, such as licensing requirements, taxation, and anti-money laundering measures, impact the crypto industry and user activities.

Tax Implications of Cryptocurrency Transactions:

Cryptocurrency transactions have tax implications that vary across jurisdictions. We discussed how governments classify cryptocurrencies for tax purposes, how capital gains are calculated, and the importance of keeping accurate records for tax reporting.

A Global Perspective on Crypto Regulations:

We examined the varied approaches to cryptocurrency regulations worldwide, ranging from supportive and innovation-friendly frameworks to strict measures aimed at risk mitigation. The diverse regulatory landscape impacts crypto adoption, market dynamics, and investment climate in different countries.

Common Security Threats in the Crypto Space:

The rise of cryptocurrencies has attracted cybercriminals, leading to various security threats. We discussed common security risks, such as phishing attacks, exchange hacks, and Ponzi schemes, and provided tips for safeguarding digital assets.

Best Practices for Securing Your Cryptocurrencies: We offered comprehensive security best practices to protect digital assets, including using hardware wallets, enabling two-factor authentication, and maintaining strong passwords. Proper security measures can mitigate risks and ensure the safety of cryptocurrency holdings.

Recognizing and Avoiding Scams and Frauds in Investing Cryptocurrencies:

Scams and frauds pose significant risks to investors in the crypto space. We highlighted red flags and warning signs to help readers recognize and avoid fraudulent schemes, protecting them from potential losses.

How Cryptocurrencies Are Used in Everyday Transactions:

We explored the growing use of cryptocurrencies for everyday transactions, including online purchases, travel, charity donations, and gaming. As adoption increases, cryptocurrencies have the potential to become mainstream payment methods alongside traditional fiat currencies.

The Role of Cryptocurrencies in Remittances and Cross-Border Payments:

We examined how cryptocurrencies disrupt the remittance industry, providing a more efficient and cost-effective substitute to traditional cross-border payment systems. Cryptocurrencies offer faster settlement times and lower fees, benefiting millions of remittance recipients worldwide.

Cryptocurrencies in the Gaming Industry and Other Applications:

We explored the integration of cryptocurrencies in the gaming industry, where they facilitate virtual asset ownership, in-game purchases, and enhanced player experiences. Additionally, we discussed other innovative applications of blockchain technology in domains such as supply chain management, healthcare, identity verification, and voting systems.

Potential Challenges and Obstacles to Mainstream Adoption of Cryptocurrencies:

We acknowledged potential challenges and obstacles to the widespread adoption of cryptocurrencies, such as regulatory uncertainties, scalability issues, technological complexities, and user education. Overcoming these challenges will be crucial for realizing the full capability of cryptocurrencies and blockchain technology.

Emerging Trends and Technologies in the Crypto Space:

We touched upon emerging trends and technologies that shape the future of the crypto space, including decentralized finance (DeFi), non-fungible tokens (NFTs), layer-2 solutions, and interoperability protocols. These innovations have the potential to drive adoption and decentralization further.

The Influence of Central Bank Digital Currencies (CBDCs) in the Crypto Space:

We explored how the concept of central bank digital currencies (CBDCs) could reshape the crypto space, blending elements of traditional fiat currencies and cryptocurrencies. CBDCs may impact financial systems, user adoption, and the future of digital payments.

Understanding the Broader Applications of Blockchain Technology:

Finally, we discussed the broader applications of blockchain technology beyond cryptocurrencies. Supply chain management, healthcare, voting, and identity verification are just a few of the industries that blockchain's decentralization, security, and transparency can revolutionize.

Throughout this book, we embarked on a comprehensive journey through cryptocurrencies and blockchain technology. We covered foundational concepts, historical backgrounds, key characteristics, benefits, and various types of cryptocurrencies. We explored the broader applications of blockchain technology, from finance to supply chain management, healthcare, and identity verification.

Additionally, we discussed the challenges and risks associated with cryptocurrencies and best practices for securing digital assets and recognizing potential scams. We emphasized the significance of regulations, their impact on the crypto industry, and tax implications for cryptocurrency transactions.

The future of cryptocurrencies and blockchain technology remains dynamic and promising. As technological advancements, market trends, and regulatory landscapes evolve, the transformative potential of cryptocurrencies continues to grow. By staying informed and adopting responsible practices, readers can effectively navigate the crypto space, harness its opportunities, and contribute to the ongoing revolution in the financial and technological realms.

Encouragement for further exploration of the crypto space

As we conclude this comprehensive book on "Decoding Cryptocurrency: Navigating the Crypto Space - An Introduction to Virtual Money and Blockchain Technology," we want to extend our encouragement for further exploration of the crypto space. Throughout this journey, we have covered the foundational concepts of cryptocurrencies, the transformative potential of blockchain technology, and the diverse applications of digital assets. Cryptocurrencies and decentralized finance (DeFi) continuously evolve, presenting many opportunities and challenges. In this section, we aim to inspire readers to continue their exploration of the crypto space, staying informed about the most current developments and embracing the possibilities that this disruptive technology offers.

The crypto space is a dynamic and quickly evolving landscape. New cryptocurrencies, DeFi protocols, and blockchain projects are constantly emerging, each offering unique use cases and innovations. By keeping up with the latest developments, readers can gain insights into cutting-edge technologies and identify opportunities for investment and participation.

One of the most compelling aspects of the crypto space is its potential to democratize finance. Cryptocurrencies and DeFi platforms empower individuals worldwide with access to financial services, irrespective of location or socioeconomic status. Users can participate in the global financial ecosystem through decentralized lending, borrowing, and earning opportunities, reducing reliance on traditional banking systems.

Cryptocurrencies can bridge financial inclusion gaps, providing the unbanked and underbanked populations with the means to access secure and transparent financial services. Readers can create a more equitable and inclusive financial landscape by exploring and supporting projects that address financial inclusion challenges.

The crypto space is at the forefront of technological innovation. From smart contracts to NFTs, Layer-2 solutions, and cross-chain interoperability, crypto advancements continue redefining traditional paradigms. By embracing these innovations, readers can gain a deeper understanding of the potential impact of blockchain technology on various industries.

Decentralized Finance (DeFi) represents a significant disruption to traditional financial systems. Readers can actively contribute to the growth of DeFi by participating in governance, providing liquidity to decentralized exchanges, and exploring yield farming opportunities. These contributions play a vital role in shaping the decentralized future of finance.

The crypto space is inherently global, transcending geographical borders and time zones. Engaging with the global community of crypto enthusiasts, developers, and investors can provide a diverse perspective on cryptocurrencies' potential and challenges. Readers can broaden their knowledge and build valuable connections by participating in online forums, social media communities, and blockchain conferences.

As cryptocurrencies gain mainstream attention, governments and regulatory bodies worldwide are grappling with the need for appropriate frameworks. Readers can stay informed about the evolving regulatory landscape and advocate for balanced and innovation-friendly policies that foster responsible growth in the crypto space.

While the crypto space offers exciting opportunities, it is crucial to approach it with caution and a willingness to learn. Readers are encouraged to conduct thorough research, understand investment risks, and exercise due diligence when participating in the crypto market.

Promoting a responsible crypto culture is essential for cryptocurrencies' long-term sustainability and acceptance. Encouraging transparency, accountability, and ethical practices within the crypto community can increase confidence among existing and potential participants.

The probable applications of blockchain technology go beyond finance. By exploring and supporting projects that apply blockchain to supply chain management, healthcare, voting systems, identity verification, and other sectors, readers can contribute to the broader adoption of this transformative technology.

As we end this book, we hope to leave readers inspired and encouraged to explore the crypto space further. Cryptocurrencies and blockchain technology are filled with opportunities for innovation, financial inclusion, and positive change. By staying informed, embracing technological advancements, contributing to DeFi, navigating regulatory frameworks responsibly, and fostering a culture of learning and caution, readers can actively participate in shaping the future of finance and technology.

We encourage readers to continue educating themselves about cryptocurrencies and blockchain, participate in the global crypto community, and advocate for a more inclusive and decentralized financial ecosystem. Embracing the potential of blockchain technology beyond finance and championing responsible practices will help unlock the transformative power of cryptocurrencies for a more equitable and interconnected world. Let us embrace the possibilities and challenges of the crypto space, as we embark on a journey towards a decentralized and inclusive future.

Final thoughts on the future of cryptocurrencies and blockchain

As we conclude our exploration of cryptocurrencies and blockchain technology, reflecting on the incredible journey we have taken through this transformative landscape is crucial. We have delved into the foundational concepts of cryptocurrencies, witnessed the rise of decentralized finance (DeFi), and explored the myriad applications of blockchain technology. In this section, we offer our final thoughts on the future of cryptocurrencies and blockchain, contemplating the opportunities, challenges, and potential disruptions that lie ahead. Cryptocurrencies' journey has been remarkable and unpredictable, and it is essential to remain open to the possibilities that this ever-evolving space presents.

Cryptocurrencies have come a long way since the inception of Bitcoin. With thousands of digital assets now available, each with its unique use case and value proposition, the crypto space has become a diverse and dynamic ecosystem. As technology advances, we can anticipate further innovation in scalability solutions, cross-chain interoperability, and enhanced privacy features. The evolving nature of cryptocurrencies will undoubtedly drive the adoption of digital assets as a legitimate and viable alternative to traditional financial instruments.

Decentralized Finance (DeFi) has emerged as a force to be reckoned with in the financial landscape. The rapid growth of DeFi protocols, providing users with access to lending, borrowing, and yield farming opportunities, showcases the power of blockchain technology in reshaping traditional finance. As DeFi matures, we anticipate the integration of more real-world assets, bringing additional value and liquidity to the crypto space. However, regulatory challenges and security concerns must be effectively addressed to ensure the sustainable growth of DeFi.

Cryptocurrencies and blockchain technology promise financial inclusion on a global scale. By providing access to financial services without intermediaries, cryptocurrencies empower the unbanked and underbanked populations worldwide. Embracing decentralization democratizes finance, fosters economic growth, and reduces financial inequality. The future of cryptocurrencies lies in bridging the gap between conventional finance and the decentralized world, unlocking new avenues for economic empowerment.

The role of governments in shaping the future of cryptocurrencies and blockchain cannot be overlooked. As cryptocurrencies gain mainstream attention, regulatory frameworks continuously evolve to address potential risks and consumer protection concerns. Balancing fostering innovation and mitigating risks is crucial for a sustainable and vibrant crypto ecosystem. Governments must collaborate with industry stakeholders to create a conducive environment that encourages responsible growth while safeguarding user interests.

While cryptocurrencies have primarily captured attention for their use as digital currencies, the underlying blockchain technology holds immense potential across various sectors. Blockchain's transparent, immutable, and secure nature can be harnessed in supply chain management, healthcare, voting systems, identity verification, and more. Embracing blockchain beyond finance opens doors to novel solutions that enhance efficiency, security, and trust in various industries, ultimately transforming how we conduct business and interact.

The energy-intensive nature of cryptocurrency mining has raised concerns about its environmental impact. As the crypto space continues to grow, addressing these concerns becomes paramount. The development and adoption of sustainable mining practices, coupled with the transition to more energy-efficient consensus mechanisms, can mitigate the environmental footprint of cryptocurrencies.

Educating the public about cryptocurrencies and blockchain technology is essential for fostering wider adoption and responsible participation. As more individuals enter the crypto space, understanding the risks, security best practices, and market dynamics becomes increasingly crucial. We can build a more informed and resilient crypto community by promoting user awareness and education.

The need for interoperability between blockchains and ecosystems becomes evident as the crypto space becomes more diverse. Projects that offer cross-chain solutions and interoperable protocols can potentially drive collaboration and liquidity across networks. Interoperability is a critical factor in achieving a seamless and integrated blockchain ecosystem.

The future of cryptocurrencies and blockchain is one of boundless potential and transformative possibilities. As technology continues to evolve, the world of finance and beyond will witness the disruptive power of decentralized systems. Embracing cryptocurrencies and blockchain technology requires an open mind and a willingness to navigate a constantly changing landscape. From the evolving nature of cryptocurrencies and the rise of DeFi to the quest for financial inclusion and the exploration of blockchain applications beyond finance, the journey ahead is as exciting as it is unpredictable.

We must recognize that the journey toward widespread acceptance of cryptocurrencies and blockchain technology is not without challenges. Regulatory landscapes, environmental concerns, and security risks must be effectively addressed. Education and user awareness will be critical in fostering a responsible and resilient crypto community. Governments, industry stakeholders, and users must collaborate to shape a sustainable future that embraces the transformative potential of cryptocurrencies while upholding principles of transparency, decentralization, and financial inclusion.

In conclusion, the future of cryptocurrencies and blockchain is a shared responsibility. By continuing to explore, innovate, and advocate for responsible growth, we can collectively shape a world where blockchain technology is pivotal in creating a more equitable, inclusive, and decentralized global society. As we embark on this journey, let us remain open to the possibilities and seize the opportunities.

Thank you for buying and reading/ listening to our book. If you found this book useful/ helpful please take a few minutes and leave a review on the platform where you purchased our book. Your feedback matters greatly to us.